MW00915984

# Retiring to Spain

### A Guide to Moving and Relocating to Spain

**Geoffreys Publishing**

Copyright © 2024 by Geoffreys Publishing All rights reserved.

No part of this book may be reproduced in any form or by any electronic or mechanical means, including information storage and retrieval systems, without written permission from the author, except for the use of brief quotations in a book review.

# Disclaimer

It is crucial to note that while this book aims to provide a comprehensive overview of retiring in Spain, the author is not a tax expert, legal professional, or licensed financial advisor. The information presented in this book is for general educational and informational purposes only and should not be considered as professional advice.

Tax laws, legal requirements, and financial regulations can be complex and are subject to change. Every individual's situation is unique, and what works for one person may not be appropriate for another. Therefore, it is strongly recommended that anyone considering a move to Spain should obtain professional tax, legal, and immigration advice tailored to their specific circumstances.

# Contents

Foreword   ix

1. Introduction to Spain   1
2. Planning Your Spanish Retirement   8
3. Visa and Residency Requirements   17
4. Healthcare in Spain   26
5. Finding Your New Home in Spain   35
6. Managing Finances in Spain   43
7. Adapting to Daily Life in Spain   51
8. Embracing Spanish Culture   59
9. Staying Connected with Family and Friends   67
10. Long-Term Considerations for Retirees in Spain   75
11. Health, Wellness, and Lifestyle in Spain   84
12. Reflections and Embracing the Journey   92

Afterword   99

# Foreword

Welcome to *Retiring to Spain: A Guide to Moving or Relocating to Spain*, your trusted companion in embarking on a transformative journey to retire in one of Europe's most captivating and vibrant countries. Whether you've long admired Spain's rich cultural tapestry, dreamt of living by the Mediterranean, or simply sought a tranquil place to enjoy your golden years, this guide offers the insights, tips, and detailed steps to help you transition smoothly and confidently into life in Spain.

Spain has become a cherished destination for retirees from all over the world. Beyond its enviable Mediterranean climate, beautiful coastlines, and historic cities, Spain offers a lifestyle that draws you in and invites you to savor life at a slower, more fulfilling pace. Here, mornings can start with a leisurely coffee in a sunlit café, afternoons with a siesta or stroll through cobbled streets, and evenings enjoying delicious local cuisine and friendly conversation. With its unparalleled quality of life, affordable cost of living, world-class health-care system, and strong sense of community, Spain is a place where retirees can find a renewed sense of purpose, adventure, and belonging.

However, moving to another country is a significant step, one that involves not only careful planning and organization but also an open mind and a willingness to adapt to a new culture and way of life. With this book, we seek to equip you with the knowledge and resources you need to make informed decisions at every stage of your relocation journey. From understanding the visa and residency process to choosing the perfect region to settle in, learning about healthcare options, managing finances, and fully embracing Spanish culture, *Retiring to Spain* is designed to guide you comprehensively and practically through each aspect of retiring abroad. This isn't just a relocation guide; it's a roadmap to a fulfilling and enriching retirement experience in one of Europe's most enchanting destinations.

As you'll discover in these pages, Spain is more than just a beautiful backdrop—it's a place that can shape your retirement years into an adventure of discovery, relaxation, and new connections. Spain's vibrant cities, such as Madrid, Barcelona, and Valencia, offer a rich blend of history, art, and modern conveniences. Coastal regions like Costa del Sol, Costa Blanca, and Costa Brava attract those who seek sunny beaches and temperate climates, while smaller, inland towns and villages provide peace, a slower pace, and close-knit communities. This diversity is part of Spain's magic: no matter your preferences or lifestyle, there's a corner of Spain that's perfectly suited for you.

This guide will also help you navigate the complexities of settling into daily life in Spain, which, while different from what you might be accustomed to, can quickly become part of your new rhythm. Life in Spain operates on its own relaxed tempo, influenced by the Spanish concept of "mañana"—a term that encourages an approach of not rushing but instead living each day fully and intentionally. In Spain, people prioritize time spent with family and friends, savored meals, and outdoor activities. Integrating into Spanish culture means embracing this way of life, adapting to the local schedules, and celebrating traditions that prioritize connection and joy.

One of the primary concerns for many retirees moving abroad is healthcare, and rightfully so. Fortunately, Spain has an excellent healthcare system that is recognized internationally for its high standards, accessibility, and affordability. Both public and private healthcare options are available, and in this guide, you'll find detailed information on navigating these systems, choosing insurance options, and ensuring your health needs are met with ease. With world-class facilities and highly trained medical professionals, Spain is well-equipped to support retirees who choose to make it their home.

Another key consideration, of course, is financial planning. Spain's cost of living is generally lower than in other Western countries, making it an attractive option for retirees looking to maximize their savings and pensions. This guide will walk you through setting up banking in Spain, managing taxes and currency, and understanding the financial implications of your move. With the right information and preparation, you'll be able to settle into a comfortable lifestyle while also budgeting for the occasional travel, hobbies, or social activities that add richness to life in Spain.

Relocating to Spain offers more than just a change of scenery; it provides the chance to expand your horizons, immerse yourself in a new language, and develop new friend-ships with people from all walks of life. The Spanish people are known for their warmth and friendliness, and many expats find it easy to build connections in their communities. Whether you're chatting with neighbors, participating in local events, or learning the language, your life in Spain can be as socially enriching as it is rewarding. Learning even basic Spanish can greatly enhance your experience, allowing you to connect more deeply with locals and immerse yourself in the culture. This guide offers practical advice for navigating language barriers and adapting to cultural nuances, so you can feel at home from the moment you arrive.

As you consider the long-term aspects of your move, such as estate planning, legal matters, and long-term healthcare, this guide will provide you with invaluable insights to help you make informed decisions about your future. Spain's systems may differ from what you're used to, but with proper guid-ance, you'll find they're designed to provide security, quality care, and legal protections that are especially relevant to retirees. These considerations may not always be the most exciting part of moving abroad, but they are essential for a stress-free and comfortable life in Spain.

Spain's diversity means that you can craft a retirement tailored precisely to your tastes, and as you turn these pages, you'll find that each chapter offers practical steps and real-istic insights to help make that vision a reality. Perhaps you envision yourself living in the cosmopolitan energy of Madrid, surrounded by art, theater, and culinary delights, or maybe it's the tranquil beauty of the Costa del Sol's beaches that draws you. Some may prefer the lush landscapes and quiet villages of the northern regions, while others are enchanted by the sun-drenched vineyards and historic architecture of Andalusia. Wherever you choose to settle, this book is your guide to navigating every step of the way, from choosing your location and securing housing to meeting residency requirements and adjusting to the Spanish way of life.

Ultimately, *Retiring to Spain* is more than a guide; it's an invitation to embrace a new way of living. Moving to Spain offers a second chapter filled with adventure, peace, and perhaps even a sense of wonder as you discover the history, landscape, and lifestyle of this beautiful country. With careful planning and an open heart, your retirement in Spain can be as rewarding as it is relaxing, as full of friendships as it is experiences. Spain's gentle pace, mild climate, and strong sense of community offer an ideal setting to focus on well-being, explore new interests, and cultivate a lifestyle that truly feels like home.

So, as you embark on this exciting journey, take a moment to picture the possibilities that await. Imagine yourself savoring a café con leche at a local café, walking along a sunlit beach, or joining in on a lively Spanish fiesta. Visualize the friendships you'll make, the places you'll discover, and the unique rhythms of life that you'll come to cherish. This book is here to support you in creating a retirement that feels rich in meaning, vibrant in experience, and wholly fulfilling.

Welcome to *Retiring to Spain: A Guide to Moving or Relocating to Spain*. May your journey be smooth, your experiences be rich, and your retirement be filled with the joys, beauty, and warmth of life in Spain. Here's to a new beginning in a land that promises endless sunshine, adventure, and the chance to live each day to its fullest. As you explore the opportunity of retiring in Spain, remember that the journey is not only about relocating but also about reinvention. Spain's welcoming spirit and vibrant culture allow retirees to not just settle but to thrive in a setting that celebrates life's simple pleasures. This is a country where relationships are nurtured, and each day brings new flavors, sights, and sounds to enjoy. In Spain, age is respected and celebrated, and you'll find yourself valued as a part of the community. Whether you're watching flamenco dancers perform to haunting Spanish guitar in Andalusia, joining locals for the harvest in La Rioja, or trying your hand at cooking paella in Valencia, retirement here is about creating memories and finding fulfillment in new ways.

Let this book serve as both your guide and your inspiration as you embrace the possibilities of life in Spain. With careful preparation, an open mind, and a spirit of curiosity, retiring in Spain can become the most enriching chapter of your life, filled with beauty, warmth, and a true sense of belonging

It is crucial to note that while this book aims to provide a comprehensive overview of retiring to Spain, the author is not a tax expert, legal professional, or licensed financial advisor. The information presented in this book is for general educational and informational purposes only and should not be considered as professional advice.

Tax laws, legal requirements, and financial regulations can be complex and are subject to change. Every individual's situation is unique, and what works for one person may not be appropriate for another. Therefore, it is strongly recommended that anyone considering a move to Spain should obtain professional tax, legal, and immigration advice tailored to their specific circumstances.

# Chapter 1
# Introduction to Spain

S pain is more than a country; it's an experience that enlivens the senses, a place where centuries of history intertwine with a vibrant, modern culture that captivates anyone who steps foot on its soil. For those contemplating retirement in this alluring part of the world, Spain offers much more than sun-soaked beaches and iconic architecture. It's a land of contrasts and deeply rooted traditions, where life unfolds at a leisurely pace, allowing one to savor every moment. Retiring to Spain isn't merely a relocation— it's a chance to rediscover a new way of life, one that celebrates both the beauty of the natural world and the richness of human connection.

Spain's appeal to retirees lies in its multifaceted charm. The country boasts diverse landscapes that shift dramatically from one region to another. In the north, the lush, green hills of Galicia offer a cool and tranquil retreat, a stark contrast to the sun-drenched shores of the Costa del Sol in the south. The eastern coast is home to the Mediterranean's gentle waves, while the rugged mountains of the Sierra Nevada tower in the distance, drawing hikers, skiers, and nature enthusiasts alike. The vast central plains provide a sense of openness and still-ness, with wide fields stretching beneath endless blue skies. Each of these regions has its unique character, cuisine, dialect, and way of life, creating a tapestry of experiences that offer something for every taste and lifestyle.

As retirees seek out Spain as a destination to spend their golden years, they often find themselves drawn to the coun-try's legendary Mediterranean climate. Spain enjoys over 3,000 hours of sunshine annually, making it one of the sunniest countries in Europe. Its climate varies depending on the region, yet it remains mild throughout the year, especially in coastal areas where winters are moderate, and summers are warm without being overly humid. This gentle climate not only fosters an outdoor lifestyle but also promotes a sense of wellbeing, as countless studies have shown the health benefits associated with sunshine and warmth. The longer days, particularly during spring and summer, provide ample time to indulge in Spain's outdoor culture, whether through beach-side relaxation, leisurely park strolls, or exploration of ancient ruins under a wide, blue sky.

For many who have already made the leap, the allure of Spain isn't only found in its landscapes or favorable weather—it's in the lifestyle. Spanish culture embraces a balance between work and leisure that fosters community, joy, and health. The Spanish day is punctuated by the famous siesta, a mid-after-noon break where shops close and people retreat from the day's heat. In Spain, lunch is a time to pause, savor food, and enjoy conversations. Evening gatherings, often around long tables set in the warm glow of outdoor lamps, create a relaxed social rhythm where food, wine, and laughter flow freely. Meals are a time for connection, with friends and family members gathering to discuss the day, celebrate special occasions, or simply enjoy each other's company. In Spain, time is a gift to be shared, not a commodity to be managed, and this approach to daily life is a deeply ingrained part of Spanish culture that retirees find both refreshing and fulfilling.

Spanish cuisine, widely considered one of the world's finest, is another aspect of life that entices those looking to retire in Spain. From the world-renowned tapas, where small plates of delicious dishes are shared communally, to the hearty stews and rice dishes of the northern regions, Spain offers a culinary adventure that is deeply rooted in tradition and regional pride. Tapas themselves are more than just food—they are a social ritual, an invitation to pause and appreciate life's pleasures. Spaniards often say that a meal is meant to be enjoyed with others, and this ethos is evident in everything from the smallest village tapas bar to the finest dining establishments. Each region contributes its own signature flavors and ingredients, reflecting its natural environment and cultural heritage. The Catalan coast, for instance, is famous for its seafood, while the heartland of Spain is known for its robust stews and cured meats. And of course, no mention of Spanish cuisine would be complete without the famed paella of Valencia, a dish as vibrant and flavorful as the country itself.

However, Spain's richness goes beyond its cuisine; it lies in its history and culture, which span millennia. With each turn of a street corner or hilltop village, one is reminded of Spain's complex past—a tapestry woven from the influences of the Romans, Visigoths, Moors, and Catholics, all of whom left their indelible marks on the land. This cultural depth is a major draw for retirees who value history, art, and architecture. Spain's cities are home to iconic structures like the Alhambra in Granada, a palace and fortress that exemplifies the grandeur of Islamic art, or the Sagrada Familia in Barcelona, Antoni Gaudí's surreal masterpiece that defies conventional architecture. Walking through the narrow, winding streets of the medieval quarter in Seville, or strolling under the aqueduct of Segovia, one feels a connection to the generations who have walked these paths before. Each region holds a different part of Spain's story, from the Roman ruins of Tarragona to the Gothic splendor of Toledo, creating endless opportunities for exploration and learning.

Beyond these historical treasures, Spain's artistic heritage continues to thrive, offering retirees a vibrant cultural scene. In major cities like Madrid and Barcelona, world-class museums such as the Prado and the Reina Sofía house masterpieces by renowned Spanish artists like Velázquez, Goya, Picasso, and Miró. The flamenco music and dance of Andalusia express the soulful passion of Spanish identity, a tradition that has survived for centuries and continues to captivate audiences worldwide. Festivals, too, play a significant role in Spanish life, with each town and village hosting its own annual celebrations, many of which are steeped in local traditions and religious observance. Some of the most famous include the Running of the Bulls in Pamplona, La Tomatina in Buñol, and Semana Santa in Seville. These festivals provide retirees with an immersive experience into Spanish culture, offering a chance to participate in communal celebrations that are filled with color, music, and joy.

As retirees look to settle in Spain, they find a country that is not only rich in tradition but also modern and progressive in its outlook. Spain has invested heavily in infrastructure and public services, providing its residents with excellent healthcare, efficient public transportation, and well-maintained public spaces. Spain's healthcare system, in particular, is one of the most highly rated in Europe. The country offers a combination of public and private healthcare services, making high-quality medical care accessible and affordable. For retirees, this is a significant benefit, as it ensures that their health needs are well-managed without excessive costs. Spanish hospitals and clinics are staffed by highly trained medical professionals, many of whom speak English, especially in regions popular with international residents. This accessibility to healthcare, combined with Spain's emphasis on wellness and the Mediterranean diet, contributes to the country's high life expectancy and quality of life.

Financially, Spain presents an appealing option for retirees. The cost of living in Spain is relatively affordable compared to other Western European nations and North America, especially when it comes to housing and daily expenses. Many retirees find that their pensions go much further in Spain, allowing them to live comfortably without compromising on lifestyle. Housing options range from chic city apartments to countryside fincas, and Spain's real estate market offers a variety of properties to suit every taste and budget. Even in popular regions like the Costa Blanca or the Balearic Islands, one can find homes at reasonable prices, often with the added benefit of beautiful views and proximity to the sea. The affordability of daily life in Spain—whether groceries, dining out, or transportation—means that retirees can enjoy a high quality of life without financial strain.

One of the most rewarding aspects of moving to Spain as a retiree is the opportunity to immerse oneself in a culture that celebrates togetherness and community. Spanish people are famously warm, open, and welcoming, particularly to those who show an interest in their customs and language. While many Spaniards, especially in urban areas, speak English, learning even a few phrases in Spanish can go a long way in building connections and gaining respect. The Spanish language is deeply expressive, and understanding it opens doors to richer interactions and a deeper connection with the people and culture of Spain. Retirees often find that their neighbors are eager to include them in local festivities, and friendships can be easily formed over shared meals and conversations in the village plaza. Spain's communal spirit makes it an ideal place for those looking to build meaningful relationships and feel a sense of belonging.

Retiring to Spain offers the chance to live a life that is both enriching and rejuvenating. The rhythm of life here is one that prioritizes personal enjoyment and connection, where every day can be filled with small but meaningful pleasures. From morning walks through sun-dappled parks to evenings spent sipping wine on a terrace, Spain encourages its residents to live fully in each moment. The Spanish term "tranquilo," often used to reassure or comfort, reflects this philosophy—it's a gentle reminder to stay calm, take things as they come, and not worry too much about the future. For retirees who may have spent years in fast-paced environments, the opportunity to slow down and embrace this approach to life can be transformative, offering a path to a more peaceful and contented retirement.

The decision to retire abroad is a deeply personal one, and while the practical aspects are important, the emotional journey of moving to a new country should not be overlooked. Spain is a land of contrasts, and newcomers may experience a range of emotions as they settle in. There is the excitement of discovery and the joy of new experiences, but there can also be moments of homesickness or cultural adjustment. Spain's slower pace of life and sometimes flexible approach to time—where appointments are often approximate and processes are not always efficient—can require an adjustment for those used to a more regimented system. However, it is precisely these differences that add to the richness of the experience. Retirees who embrace the quirks of Spanish life often find that they grow personally and gain new perspectives that bring a deeper sense of satisfaction and resilience.

For those who do choose to retire in Spain, the journey is one of continual discovery and delight. From the snow-capped peaks of the Pyrenees to the golden sands of the Canary Islands, from bustling markets in Barcelona to tranquil vineyards in La Rioja, Spain is a country that invites exploration at every turn. There is always something new to see, taste, and experience, and the chance to continue learning and growing well into one's retirement years. Retiring to Spain means embracing a lifestyle that celebrates the beauty of the moment, the strength of community, and the joy of simple pleasures. It's a country where life is lived fully, whether through shared meals, community festivals, or quiet moments in nature.

In Spain, retirees find not just a new home, but a new way of being—one that is as vibrant, diverse, and welcoming as the country itself. This book will guide you through every step of this journey, providing the insights and tools you need to make Spain your own. Whether you're drawn by the Mediterranean's blue waters, the history embedded in every city, or the chance to live at a more leisurely pace, Spain is ready to welcome you with open arms, promising a retirement filled with warmth, discovery, and the simple joys of a life well-lived.

# Chapter 2
# Planning Your Spanish Retirement

P lanning a retirement in Spain is an exciting journey that combines dreams with practical steps, balancing aspiration with detailed preparation. Moving to another country for retirement requires deep consideration, not just about where you'll live but how you'll live, who you'll connect with, and what kind of life you want to create. Spain offers a remarkable array of experiences and environments, from coastal retreats to vibrant cities and peaceful villages. The process of relocating involves understanding both the broad landscape and the finer details, ensuring that you're ready to make the most of this significant life transition.

As you embark on planning your Spanish retirement, the first step is an honest self-assessment. Ask yourself why Spain appeals to you as a retirement destination, beyond the allure of its sunlit coastlines and rich cultural heritage. Many retirees are drawn to Spain's slower pace of life and warm Mediterranean lifestyle, but the process is about more than just finding a new address. It's about embracing a lifestyle shift, one that involves adapting to new customs, making new friends, and learning a new language. For some, Spain represents a lifelong dream to live in a country steeped in history, with a lifestyle centered around family, friends, and the enjoyment of simple pleasures. For others, it's an opportunity to step back from the fast-paced life they've known and rediscover themselves in a peaceful, inspiring environment. Recognizing what drives you personally will help you stay grounded and focused as you navigate the practicalities of moving to a new country.

For many retirees, an exploratory trip is a valuable way to get a firsthand feel for life in Spain. An extended stay, lasting several weeks or even months, can provide invaluable insights that no amount of online research can replace. During this time, take the opportunity to explore several regions, keeping an open mind and observing not only the scenery but the daily rhythms of life in each area. Some may be drawn to the bustling cities of Madrid and Barcelona, where cultural attractions, nightlife, and urban amenities abound. Others may find a quieter joy in smaller towns like Ronda or Alicante, where life moves at a gentler pace, and a sense of close-knit community is palpable. An extended visit allows you to immerse yourself in the places that might become your new home, observing how you feel in each environment, whether it's the cosmopolitan energy of a city or the relaxed tranquility of a coastal village. A visit of this kind can help you solidify your vision and clarify what you truly want from your retirement in Spain.

During your exploratory stay, observe not just the picturesque highlights but the practical aspects of daily life. Pay attention to things like transportation options, grocery shopping, access to healthcare facilities, and the availability of social and recreational activities. Consider how easy it is to get around without a car if you prefer not to drive, and familiarize yourself with Spain's extensive public transport system, including buses, trams, and high-speed trains. These details might seem minor at first, but they play a significant role in shaping your day-to-day experience and can determine whether a location is truly compatible with your lifestyle and needs. Speak to other retirees and locals, if possible, to get a sense of the community and to learn from their experiences. Their insights can provide valuable information about what it's really like to live in Spain, including potential challenges and solutions for adapting to the culture.

One of the key considerations in planning a Spanish retirement is financial readiness. Spain is known for its affordable cost of living compared to other Western European countries, but it's essential to understand the financial implications of living there as an expat. First, assess your sources of income and determine how they will be affected by your move. If you rely on pensions, social security, or investment income, research how each of these will be impacted by relocating to Spain. Some countries, like the United States, have agreements with Spain regarding pension payments, but it's crucial to verify how your specific financial situation aligns with Spanish and international regulations. Many retirees find that their pensions and savings stretch further in Spain, allowing them to enjoy a comfortable lifestyle without the financial strain they might experience in their home countries.

Once you have a clear picture of your income sources, it's time to develop a realistic budget that reflects the cost of living in Spain. Housing is likely to be one of your most significant expenses, whether you choose to rent or buy. In popular regions like the Costa del Sol or Costa Blanca, property prices can be higher due to demand from international residents, while rural areas and smaller towns may offer more affordable options. Consider not only the cost of acquiring property but also maintenance costs, utilities, and property taxes, as well as any additional costs associated with home ownership in Spain. If you choose to rent, research the rental market in your desired area to ensure it aligns with your budget and lifestyle. Utilities such as electricity, water, and internet vary depending on location and usage but are generally reasonable, particularly compared to countries with high utility costs.

Beyond housing, think about the everyday costs of groceries, dining out, transportation, and healthcare. Spain offers excellent value for dining and groceries, especially if you embrace local markets and seasonal produce. Dining out is affordable, with many local restaurants offering "menú del día" options —set menus that provide a filling meal at a budget-friendly price. Public transportation is both efficient and economical, particularly in urban areas, and many retirees find they can live comfortably without a car. However, if you enjoy driving or plan to live in a more remote area, consider the costs of fuel, insurance, and vehicle maintenance. Healthcare costs are another vital consideration. While Spain's healthcare system is high-quality and generally affordable, having comprehensive health insurance is essential for peace of mind and to ensure access to private care if needed.

For many retirees, managing finances in Spain involves more than just budgeting for everyday expenses; it requires a sound understanding of tax obligations. Spain has specific tax laws for residents and non-residents, and understanding these distinctions is crucial. Retirees planning to stay in Spain for more than 183 days per year will likely be considered tax residents, which means they may be subject to Spanish taxes on global income. This can impact pensions, investment income, and other sources of revenue, so consulting with a financial advisor or tax professional with expertise in Spanish tax law is highly advisable. Additionally, Spain offers the "Beckham Law" or "Regimen Fiscal Especial para Traba-jadores Desplazados," which provides tax breaks for foreign residents in certain circumstances, though it's primarily geared towards workers rather than retirees. Understanding your tax obligations early on can help you avoid surprises and ensure that your finances are structured optimally for your new life in Spain.

As you move forward in your planning, creating a detailed timeline is invaluable. Consider starting your preparations at least a year before your intended move date, as this allows you ample time to address each step thoroughly. Begin by intensifying your research, not only about the specific area you're interested in but also about any legal or financial requirements that apply to your situation. A timeline also allows you to organize tasks like decluttering, selling, or storing belongings you won't be taking with you. Many retirees find that simplifying their possessions before a move offers a sense of freedom, allowing them to embrace their new life unburdened by excess belongings. Use this time to prioritize what matters most, whether it's treasured heirlooms, essential furniture, or sentimental items that you want to bring with you.

The visa process is another critical aspect of planning your retirement in Spain. Spain offers several visa options, with the Non-Lucrative Visa being one of the most common choices for retirees who do not intend to work. This visa requires proof of sufficient income or savings to support yourself, and the application process can take several months, so it's wise to begin gathering the necessary documents well in advance. The Golden Visa, which requires a significant investment in Spanish real estate or business, is another option that may appeal to those with the means to make a substantial financial commitment. Whichever visa option you choose, ensure you fully understand the requirements and have all documentation prepared before applying, as incomplete applications can lead to delays or complications.

Healthcare is a top priority for most retirees, and Spain's healthcare system is one of the factors that make it an attractive retirement destination. The country offers both public and private healthcare options, with many expats finding the public system to be of high quality and affordable. However, most retirees choose to supplement with private health insurance to ensure access to a broader range of services and shorter wait times. Spain's public healthcare system provides coverage for residents, but access to the system depends on obtaining a residency visa. It's essential to research health insurance options early in your planning process, comparing international and local providers to find a policy that best meets your needs. Many health insurance providers offer specific plans for expatriates that include English-speaking customer service, direct billing with hospitals, and coverage for pre-existing conditions, all of which can provide peace of mind as you settle into your new life in Spain.

As you consider healthcare, take time to think about your long-term needs, including aging-in-place services, access to specialists, and the availability of facilities for chronic health conditions. Spain's healthcare system generally provides excellent care for seniors, but if you have specific medical needs, it's wise to research the availability of relevant services in your chosen area. Some retirees prefer to live in or near larger cities, where hospitals and specialist clinics are more accessible. For those interested in alternative treatments, Spain also offers a range of holistic health services, including acupuncture, osteopathy, and herbal medicine, which may complement traditional medical care.

Learning the language is another essential aspect of preparing for life in Spain. While many Spaniards in urban areas and tourist destinations speak English, particularly younger generations, learning Spanish opens doors to deeper cultural immersion and more meaningful interactions with locals. Starting with basic conversational Spanish can help you navigate daily activities, from ordering food to asking for directions, and it demonstrates respect for the culture, which locals appreciate. Many retirees find language learning to be a stimulating and rewarding activity, one that keeps their minds engaged while also fostering a sense of belonging in their new home. Consider enrolling in a language course or practicing with a tutor, whether in person or online, to build your confidence and proficiency over time.

One of the most fulfilling parts of preparing for a retirement in Spain is envisioning your future lifestyle and the activities that will bring joy and meaning to your days. Spain offers countless opportunities for enrichment, whether through art, music, sports, or community involvement. Take some time to reflect on the interests you want to pursue and the hobbies you may want to try. Spain's outdoor culture encourages an active lifestyle, with activities like hiking, golfing, and cycling widely accessible and popular among retirees. Many cities and towns also offer cultural classes, from flamenco dance to Spanish cooking, providing an enjoyable way to learn more about the local heritage while meeting people who share your interests.

Spain's social culture is warm and inclusive, making it easy for retirees to build connections and friendships. Community activities, volunteer opportunities, and expat groups provide avenues for meeting new people and establishing a support network. Many towns with significant expat populations have organizations specifically geared towards helping new residents acclimate and find community. These groups can be a valuable resource for learning about local events, finding reliable service providers, and navigating any challenges you may encounter. Building a social network not only enhances your enjoyment of life in Spain but also provides a support system that can be invaluable as you adapt to your new environment.

Planning a retirement in Spain is ultimately about creating a lifestyle that balances leisure with purpose. It's an opportunity to redefine what your retirement years will look like, to choose a place where you feel both inspired and at home. Spain's unique blend of history, culture, and modern amenities offers an ideal setting for those seeking to make the most of this stage in life. Whether you envision a life filled with art and culture, quiet days by the sea, or an active, outdoor lifestyle, Spain provides the framework to bring your retirement dreams to life.

As you plan and prepare, remember that the journey to Spain is as much an emotional one as it is logistical. Moving to a new country involves stepping out of your comfort zone and embracing the unknown. With thoughtful planning, an open heart, and a willingness to learn and adapt, your retirement in Spain can be the beginning of a beautiful new chapter, one filled with experiences, friendships, and memories that will enrich your life for years to come.

# Chapter 3
# Visa and Residency Requirements

Navigating the visa and residency requirements for Spain is an essential part of preparing for a successful and enjoyable retirement. While Spain warmly welcomes retirees from around the world, it has specific procedures that must be followed to establish legal residency, allowing you to stay for extended periods and enjoy all the benefits that come with being a resident. The process might seem daunting at first, with different visa types, income requirements, and application procedures to consider. However, with careful planning and a clear understanding of what's required, you can secure the right visa and residency status smoothly, ensuring that your time in Spain is legally compliant and free from bureaucratic stress.

For most retirees, the process of moving to Spain begins with choosing the appropriate visa. Spain offers several options for long-term stays, and the most common visa for retirees is the Non-Lucrative Visa. This visa is designed specifically for non-working individuals who can demonstrate that they have sufficient financial resources to support themselves without needing employment. It's an ideal choice for retirees who plan to live off their pension, savings, or other income sources. The Non-Lucrative Visa is particularly appealing because it allows for long-term residency and can be renewed, providing a stable pathway for those who wish to make Spain their primary home.

The Non-Lucrative Visa requires applicants to meet several financial and legal criteria. To qualify, you'll need to show proof of adequate income or savings that can sustain your life in Spain. Generally, this means having a monthly income of around 2,259 euros for an individual, with additional funds required for each dependent. This financial requirement aims to ensure that you won't need to work or rely on Spanish social assistance. Many retirees find that their pensions or retirement savings satisfy this requirement comfortably, but it's crucial to confirm the specific amount required, as this figure can vary slightly depending on the current regulations and exchange rates.

In addition to proving financial solvency, you'll need to provide other essential documents, including a valid passport, a completed application form, and recent passport-sized photos. One of the more complex requirements is a criminal background check from your home country. This background check must be recent and authenticated, often through a process called an apostille, which is a form of international certification. Depending on your home country, obtaining a background check can take several weeks, so it's advisable to start this step early in your application process. You'll also need a medical certificate stating that you do not have any contagious diseases that could pose a public health risk. This requirement is straightforward but can require specific word-ing, so it's wise to consult with your Spanish consulate or embassy for exact details.

Once you have gathered all necessary documents, you'll need to submit your application at the Spanish consulate or embassy in your home country. The Non-Lucrative Visa application cannot be processed within Spain, so planning your application timeline is essential, especially if you're managing an international move and coordinating the sale of a property or the shipment of belongings. After you submit your application, you may need to attend an in-person appointment at the consulate or embassy, where officials will review your documentation and may ask questions to clarify your plans and financial status. The processing time can vary, but most applicants receive a response within one to three months, though it's advisable to prepare for potential delays.

Upon approval, the Non-Lucrative Visa allows you to enter Spain and stay for up to 90 days, during which you'll need to apply for your residency card, known as the Tarjeta de Iden-tidad de Extranjero (TIE). This card is critical as it formalizes your residency status and is required for access to services like healthcare and banking. To apply for the TIE, you'll visit your local Oficina de Extranjeros (Foreigner's Office) in Spain. This part of the process includes submitting fingerprints, showing your visa, and presenting proof of address within Spain, often through a rental agreement or property deed. After this appointment, you'll typically receive a temporary TIE card, followed by a permanent card after several weeks.

The Non-Lucrative Visa is renewable annually for up to five years, after which you may be eligible for long-term residency or even citizenship if desired. Each renewal requires you to show that you still meet the financial and legal requirements, as well as evidence that you have been residing in Spain. Many retirees find the renewal process straightforward, but it's essential to track deadlines and maintain organized records, as failing to renew on time can complicate your residency status.

For those with significant financial resources who wish to invest in Spain, the Golden Visa offers another option for residency. Introduced to attract foreign investment, the Golden Visa provides residency for individuals who invest a substantial amount in Spanish real estate, businesses, or government bonds. The real estate option is particularly popular among retirees who wish to purchase a home in Spain. To qualify, you'll need to invest a minimum of 500,000 euros in Spanish property, whether it's a single property or multiple properties that together meet the threshold. The Golden Visa is attractive not only because it grants residency but also because it allows for flexibility—Golden Visa holders can travel throughout the Schengen Area without restrictions and are not required to spend a minimum amount of time in Spain each year.

In addition to property investment, the Golden Visa can also be obtained through business investments, such as creating jobs in Spain or investing in Spanish companies, as well as through substantial deposits in Spanish banks or government bonds. While the Golden Visa requires a higher initial financial commitment, it offers benefits that are particularly appealing to retirees who value flexibility, especially if they plan to divide their time between Spain and another country.

For those considering the Golden Visa, the application process is similar to the Non-Lucrative Visa but involves additional steps related to the investment itself. You'll need to provide proof of your investment, such as property purchase documents or business contracts, along with the standard requirements for identification, background checks, and health certificates. Once the Golden Visa is granted, it's valid for two years and can be renewed for additional five-year periods, making it a long-term solution for retirees who want to maintain Spanish residency without committing to full-time residence requirements.

Another important aspect of Spanish residency is understanding the tax implications. Spain has specific tax laws for residents, and becoming a tax resident in Spain may affect your income, pensions, and investments. Spanish residents are subject to Spanish income tax on their global income, which means that pensions, rental income, investment returns, and other earnings may be taxable in Spain. To avoid double taxation, Spain has tax treaties with many countries, including the United States, the United Kingdom, and Canada, which can prevent you from being taxed twice on the same income. It's highly advisable to consult with a tax professional who specializes in Spanish taxation for expatriates, as tax laws can be complex and subject to change.

One program that may be beneficial for some retirees is the "Regimen Fiscal Especial para Trabajadores Desplazados," also known as the Beckham Law. Originally designed for foreign workers in Spain, this program can offer significant tax reductions under specific conditions, although it's not always applicable for retirees. Those who qualify for the Beckham Law may be taxed on only their Spanish-source income, rather than their global income, for up to six years.

This program has strict eligibility requirements, so it's essential to understand whether it applies to your situation and to consult with a tax advisor who can guide you through the details.

The concept of "Empadronamiento" is another important part of the residency process in Spain. This is the act of registering with the local town hall or city council in the municipality where you reside, and it serves as proof of your address in Spain. Being "empadronado" is essential for various administrative purposes, such as accessing healthcare, enrolling in local services, and even voting in local elections if you later qualify. Registering in the municipal register is generally a straightforward process; you'll need to bring proof of residence, such as a rental agreement or property deed, along with your passport and visa. The Empadronamiento is often overlooked by new residents, but it's a legal requirement, and being registered can simplify many aspects of daily life in Spain.

Healthcare is another critical consideration for retirees moving to Spain, and residency status plays a significant role in determining your healthcare options. As a resident of Spain, you may be eligible to access Spain's public healthcare system, known as the Sistema Nacional de Salud (SNS). The SNS is funded through taxes and offers high-quality medical care that is widely accessible and generally affordable. However, non-EU residents typically need to have private health insurance or meet specific conditions before qualifying for public healthcare. Many retirees opt for private health insurance that offers direct access to private hospitals and clinics, shorter wait times, and English-speaking staff. Private insurance providers in Spain offer various packages tailored to the needs of expatriates, making it easy to find a plan that suits your medical needs and budget.

Residency in Spain also opens the door to various social benefits, including access to public services, educational opportunities, and cultural activities. As a resident, you'll have the right to enjoy Spain's many public services, from libraries and parks to community centers and local events. Spain's focus on community and well-being means that local municipalities often provide free or low-cost activities for residents, including exercise classes, art workshops, language courses, and more. Participating in these activities can be a wonderful way to integrate into the community, meet new people, and enrich your retirement experience.

For those interested in becoming fully integrated into Spanish society, the option of obtaining permanent residency or citizenship is worth exploring. After five years of continuous legal residence in Spain, you may be eligible to apply for permanent residency. This status grants you the same rights as other residents, with the added benefit of not having to renew your residency card as frequently. Permanent residency is particularly appealing to retirees who have built a life in Spain and plan to remain there indefinitely. To apply for permanent residency, you'll need to show proof of legal residence over the five-year period, often through documentation such as rental agreements, utility bills, and official records from the Oficina de Extranjeros.

For retirees who wish to fully commit to life in Spain, citizenship is an option after ten years of continuous legal residence. Spanish citizenship offers the right to vote in national elections, and it can simplify travel within the European Union. However, Spain does not allow dual citizenship for most non-

EU nationals, which means you may need to renounce your original citizenship to become a Spanish citizen. The decision to pursue citizenship is a significant one, and it's not necessary to enjoy the benefits of life in Spain. Many retirees are content with permanent residency, which provides long-term stability without the complexities of citizenship.

As you move through the process of securing your visa and residency status, it's essential to stay organized and proactive. Each step requires specific documentation, and timelines can vary based on consulate availability, processing times, and any additional requirements. Create a checklist and set reminders for each phase, from gathering documents to scheduling appointments and renewing your residency card. Maintaining copies of all documents and organizing them in a dedicated folder can streamline the process and reduce stress if you need to reference previous applications or renewals.

Living as a resident in Spain offers a level of stability and security that enhances the retirement experience. By understanding the visa and residency requirements and taking the time to meet each requirement thoughtfully, you can lay a strong foundation for your new life in Spain. This chapter has provided an overview of the Non-Lucrative Visa, the Golden Visa, tax considerations, healthcare access, and the pathway to permanent residency or citizenship. These elements form the legal framework that supports your stay in Spain, allowing you to enjoy your retirement without legal uncertainties.

Spain's welcoming approach to retirees, combined with its high quality of life and rich cultural heritage, makes it an ideal place to begin this new chapter. Whether you're drawn to the vibrant energy of its cities or the tranquility of its coastal towns, Spain is ready to welcome you into its diverse communities. The visa and residency process, though complex, is a necessary step toward achieving a life of fulfillment, adventure, and contentment in a country that values community, history, and the beauty of everyday life. Embrace this journey with patience and optimism, knowing that each requirement brings you closer to making Spain your home.

## Chapter 4
# Healthcare in Spain

ealthcare is one of the most crucial considerations for retirees choosing to relocate, and Spain offers a healthcare system that is both comprehensive and accessible. For retirees planning to spend their golden years in Spain, understanding the country's healthcare system is essential for ensuring that your medical needs are well cared for in a foreign country. Spain's healthcare system is internationally renowned for its high quality, affordability, and accessibility. The system includes both public and private healthcare options, giving residents access to a wide range of services, from routine check-ups and preventive care to specialized treatments and surgeries. Spain's approach to healthcare not only ensures that residents can receive necessary care when needed but also reflects the country's emphasis on community well-being and quality of life.

Spain's healthcare system is a hybrid model, combining a universal public healthcare system with a robust private sector. The public healthcare system, known as the Sistema Nacional de Salud (SNS), provides universal coverage to all residents and citizens, funded by taxes. This system operates under the principle that healthcare is a right, not a privilege, and it aims to provide medical services to anyone who needs them, regardless of their economic situation. The SNS covers the vast majority of healthcare needs, including primary care, specialist consultations, hospitalization, and emergency care. In addition to primary and emergency services, the SNS offers mental health services, rehabilitation, and even some forms of long-term care. The public healthcare system is often viewed as a national treasure, one that reflects Spain's commitment to equitable healthcare access for all residents.

For retirees moving to Spain, access to the public healthcare system depends on residency status. European Union (EU) citizens who are residents in Spain automatically qualify for public healthcare, as Spain is a member of the EU and adheres to the regulations of the European Health Insurance Card (EHIC). This means that EU citizens who retire to Spain can generally access public healthcare with minimal obstacles. However, for non-EU retirees, accessing the public healthcare system requires either a residency visa that grants healthcare access or the purchase of private health insurance. Spain has specific visa requirements for non-EU residents that often mandate proof of private health insurance before residency is granted. This requirement ensures that new residents have a means of covering their medical costs without relying on public resources until they qualify for public healthcare after a set period.

Private health insurance in Spain plays a critical role for retirees, particularly during the initial period of residency before qualifying for public healthcare. Spain's private healthcare sector is extensive and widely regarded for its high standards, modern facilities, and skilled professionals. Private health insurance offers several advantages, including shorter wait times, greater flexibility in choosing healthcare providers, and access to private hospitals and clinics. For many retirees, private health insurance provides peace of mind, knowing they can access top-tier medical care quickly and conveniently. Numerous private insurers in Spain cater specifically to expatriates, offering English-speaking support, comprehensive coverage options, and direct billing arrangements with hospitals and clinics. These plans often include coverage for routine care, hospitalization, specialist consultations, and emergency services, as well as optional add-ons like dental and vision care.

The cost of private health insurance in Spain varies depending on the coverage level, age, and health status of the policyholder, but it is generally more affordable than in many other Western countries, particularly the United States. Basic private health insurance plans typically range from 50 to 200 euros per month for retirees, depending on the level of coverage. Comprehensive plans with extensive coverage options may cost more but remain accessible to most retirees on a fixed income. Spain's private healthcare system provides an excellent supplement to the public system, allowing retirees to choose the level of care that best suits their needs and preferences. Many retirees start with private health insurance and, once eligible, transition to the public system or maintain a combination of both, using private insurance for certain specialized or non-essential services.

Once a retiree becomes a legal resident of Spain and meets the residency requirements, they may be eligible to access the public healthcare system. The process typically involves registering with the local social security office to receive a health card, or tarjeta sanitaria, which grants access to public healthcare facilities. This card allows retirees to use public health services in the same way as Spanish citizens. The registration process is usually straightforward, but it requires proof of residency, such as a visa or residency permit, and may also require a certificate of empadronamiento, which verifies that you are registered with the local town hall. Once registered, retirees have the same rights and responsibilities as Spanish citizens within the SNS, including access to primary care physicians, specialists, emergency services, and hospital care.

The quality of healthcare in Spain is one of the reasons the country is so appealing to retirees. Spain consistently ranks high in global healthcare indices, thanks to its highly trained medical professionals, advanced facilities, and commitment to patient-centered care. Spanish doctors are well-regarded for their expertise, and many have received training abroad, particularly in the United States and the United Kingdom, which helps ensure that their skills and knowledge are up-to-date with international standards. In addition, Spain's medical facilities are modern and well-equipped, especially in major cities and regions popular with expatriates. Hospitals in Spain are subject to strict regulations and quality control measures, ensuring that patients receive high-quality care in a safe environment. This quality of care extends to smaller clinics and regional hospitals, many of which offer specialized services that cater to the needs of elderly residents.

One of the unique aspects of healthcare in Spain is its emphasis on preventive care. The SNS promotes preventive healthcare through regular screenings, vaccinations, and public health initiatives aimed at improving overall health and well-being. Primary care doctors in Spain play an essential role in preventive care, working with patients to identify and manage health risks before they develop into serious issues. For retirees, this focus on prevention is especially beneficial, as regular check-ups and screenings can help detect and manage age-related conditions early, improving health outcomes and quality of life. Spain's healthcare system also prioritizes patient education, with programs and resources that help individuals take an active role in managing their health. This proactive approach to healthcare aligns well with the needs of retirees who want to maintain their health and independence as they age.

Mental health is another important component of Spain's healthcare system, and it is integrated into both public and private healthcare options. Spanish society has become increasingly aware of mental health issues, and the SNS provides access to mental health professionals, including psychiatrists, psychologists, and counselors. Retirees have access to mental health services, whether they need support for adjusting to life in a new country, managing stress, or addressing more serious mental health conditions. In recent years, mental health support has expanded significantly, with a growing number of private clinics and telehealth options that offer mental health services in multiple languages, including English. Many expatriates find that having access to mental health resources in their native language is invaluable, as it allows them to communicate their needs and concerns more effectively. This accessibility to mental health support is especially beneficial for retirees, who may experience feelings of loneliness or homesickness as they adjust to a new culture and way of life.

One of the most appealing aspects of Spain's healthcare system is its affordability, particularly within the public sector. For retirees on a fixed income, the low cost of healthcare in Spain can make a significant difference in their quality of life. Public healthcare in Spain is funded through taxes, which means that most services are either free or available at a minimal cost for residents. For example, visits to a primary care doctor, hospitalization, and most specialist consultations are covered by the SNS with little to no out-of-pocket expenses for patients. Prescription medications are also subsidized, making them affordable for retirees who may need ongoing medication for chronic conditions. Spanish pharmacies play a key role in healthcare delivery, with pharmacists providing guidance on medication usage and answering questions about minor health concerns. Spain's pharmacies are highly accessible, even in smaller towns, and many medications are available over the counter at a fraction of the cost in other countries.

However, it is important to note that certain services, such as dental care and optical care, are not fully covered by the public healthcare system. Retirees who require regular dental check-ups or corrective lenses may need to budget for these expenses or consider a private insurance plan that includes dental and vision coverage. Many private health insurance providers in Spain offer add-ons that cover these services, allowing retirees to customize their healthcare plan based on their needs. Additionally, some retirees may choose to travel to nearby countries for certain medical procedures, as Spain's proximity to other European nations allows for "medical tourism" in regions where specific treatments may be more affordable or accessible.

For retirees with chronic health conditions, Spain's healthcare system offers various resources and programs to manage long-term illnesses. Chronic diseases, such as diabetes, hypertension, and arthritis, are managed through a combination of primary care, specialist consultations, and community-based programs that provide education and support. The SNS often assigns a primary care doctor, known as a médico de cabecera, who oversees the patient's overall health and coordinates care with specialists. This continuity of care helps retirees build a relationship with their healthcare provider, ensuring that their medical history and needs are well understood. Many local health centers offer workshops and support groups for individuals with chronic conditions, promoting a community-oriented approach to healthcare. These programs help retirees manage their conditions effectively, allowing them to maintain an active and fulfilling lifestyle.

Spain's climate and lifestyle also contribute positively to retirees' health. The Mediterranean diet, which is rich in fruits, vegetables, whole grains, olive oil, and fish, is widely considered one of the healthiest diets in the world. This diet is associated with numerous health benefits, including lower rates of heart disease, reduced inflammation, and improved mental health. Many retirees find that they naturally adopt the Mediterranean diet upon moving to Spain, as fresh produce, seafood, and healthy oils are widely available and affordable. Spain's emphasis on outdoor living, with its warm climate and abundant green spaces, also encourages an active lifestyle. Many retirees spend their days walking through town plazas, hiking in nature reserves, or swimming in the Mediterranean, all of which contribute to a balanced and healthy lifestyle. This combination of diet, physical activity, and social engagement creates a holistic approach to health that supports well-being at every age.

For those concerned about emergency medical care, Spain has a well-developed emergency response system that provides prompt and efficient care. Emergency rooms in public hospitals are equipped to handle a wide range of medical emergencies, and ambulances are available throughout the country, even in remote areas. Spain's emergency services are known for their speed and professionalism, and emergency care is free of charge for residents and visitors alike, regardless of insurance status. This aspect of the healthcare system provides retirees with the reassurance that they will receive immediate care in the event of an emergency, whether they are experiencing a minor injury or a major health crisis.

Another advantage of healthcare in Spain is the availability of alternative and complementary medicine. Many Spaniards incorporate holistic practices into their healthcare routine, and the SNS recognizes certain alternative treatments as complementary to traditional medicine. Services such as acupuncture, homeopathy, and osteopathy are available through both public and private healthcare providers, although they are often not covered by public insurance. Retirees interested in holistic health practices will find a variety of options available, especially in regions with large expatriate communities. This flexibility allows retirees to explore different approaches to health and wellness, combining traditional and alternative treatments as they see fit.

Spain's healthcare system also supports the concept of aging in place, with programs and services designed to help elderly residents maintain their independence. The country offers various home care services, including assistance with daily tasks, physical therapy, and nursing care for individuals with mobility or health challenges. Local municipalities often provide resources and support for elderly residents, including social programs, transportation services, and meal delivery for those with limited mobility. Many retirees choose to stay in their own homes as they age, and Spain's focus on community and family support makes it feasible for seniors to receive care while remaining in familiar surroundings. Aging in place is particularly attractive for retirees who wish to stay connected to their community and continue enjoying the lifestyle they've established in Spain.

As a retiree in Spain, understanding the healthcare system can provide peace of mind and a sense of security. Spain's commitment to high-quality, accessible healthcare ensures that residents are well-supported in their medical needs, allowing retirees to focus on enjoying their new life in Spain. The combination of public and private healthcare options offers flexibility, enabling retirees to choose the level of care that best suits their individual circumstances. With affordable healthcare, a focus on preventive care, and a supportive community environment, Spain provides an ideal setting for retirees who prioritize health and well-being.

Moving to a new country for retirement is a significant decision, and healthcare is a central part of that choice. Spain's healthcare system reflects the country's values of community, accessibility, and quality, offering retirees the resources and support they need to enjoy a fulfilling and healthy life. By understanding the healthcare options available, retirees can make informed decisions about their medical care, ensuring a smooth and comfortable transition into this exciting new chapter.

# Chapter 5
# Finding Your New Home in Spain

The dream of living in Spain—walking through picturesque towns, lounging under a Mediterranean sun, and calling a place with rich culture and history home—captures the imagination of many retirees. Yet, before you can fully embrace your new life in Spain, finding the right home is an essential step in making this dream a reality. Choosing where to live and selecting the type of home that best suits your needs requires careful thought and planning. Spain is a country of incredible geographic and cultural diversity, with each region offering a unique blend of lifestyle, climate, and ambiance. Whether you envision yourself in a bustling city apartment, a serene seaside villa, or a rustic countryside retreat, Spain has a location and housing style to match your desires. As you begin your search, understanding the nuances of Spain's real estate market, regional differences, and the logistics of buying or renting property will help you make informed decisions that lead to a fulfilling retirement.

One of the first decisions to consider when searching for your home in Spain is location. Spain offers a wide variety of regions, each with its own personality and appeal. The Mediterranean coast, with its sunny beaches and relaxed lifestyle, is a favorite among retirees, particularly the Costa del Sol and Costa Blanca. These coastal areas offer beautiful beaches, a mild climate, and plenty of amenities, making them popular with international residents. Towns like Marbella, Alicante, and Torrevieja are known for their expat-friendly communities, where English is widely spoken and there is a strong network of support for newcomers. The social atmosphere in these regions is inviting, with a slower pace of life that encourages outdoor activities, dining al fresco, and enjoying the natural beauty of the coastline.

For those drawn to the energy and amenities of a larger city, Spain's urban centers provide vibrant options. Madrid, the capital, offers a dynamic mix of history, culture, and modern conveniences, with world-class museums, theaters, and dining options. Barcelona, famous for its unique architecture and cosmopolitan vibe, combines the advantages of city living with proximity to the beach, giving residents the best of both worlds. While city life may be more fast-paced than the coastal regions, the wealth of cultural activities, festivals, and events in places like Madrid and Barcelona make them attractive to retirees who seek engagement and excitement in their daily lives. In both cities, excellent public transportation networks make it easy to explore without needing a car, adding to the appeal for those who prefer urban conveniences.

On the other hand, some retirees may feel most at home in Spain's charming villages and rural areas, where a slower pace of life and close-knit communities offer a sense of tranquility and connection. Regions such as Andalusia and Galicia are home to picturesque villages where life unfolds according to traditions that have been preserved for generations. Towns like Ronda, famous for its dramatic cliffs and historic architecture, or Altea, known for its white-washed buildings and scenic Mediterranean views, embody the beauty and simplicity of rural Spain. In these areas, you'll find a strong sense of community, with neighbors who look out for one another and a slower, more intentional approach to daily life. The landscape in rural areas is often breathtaking, with olive groves, vineyards, and mountains creating a serene backdrop. Living in the countryside can be ideal for retirees who wish to escape the hustle and bustle and immerse themselves in nature, away from the pressures of city living.

As you consider where you want to live, climate plays an important role. Spain has a diverse climate that varies significantly from one region to another. The Mediterranean coast enjoys a mild climate year-round, with hot summers and mild winters, making it ideal for those who appreciate warm weather. The northwestern regions, such as Galicia and Asturias, have a cooler, wetter climate, reminiscent of the verdant landscapes found in Ireland or the UK. Central Spain, including Madrid and Castilla-La Mancha, experiences hot summers and cold winters due to its high altitude and inland location. Each climate offers unique advantages, but understanding the seasonal weather patterns in your chosen area will help you prepare for the year-round experience of living there.

Once you have chosen a region, deciding between renting and buying is the next step in the process. Each option has its advantages and challenges, depending on your goals, budget, and level of commitment. For retirees who are new to Spain, renting may be an appealing option, as it provides flexibility to explore different areas and decide on a long-term location. Renting also allows you to experience the local lifestyle without the responsibilities of homeownership, which can be particularly beneficial if you are unsure about which region or type of home best suits you. Spain's rental market is robust, with a range of properties available, from furnished apartments in city centers to standalone villas in coastal and rural areas. Rental contracts in Spain can vary, but most are for one-year terms, with the option to renew annually. Monthly rental costs depend on the location, with higher prices in major cities like Madrid and Barcelona, and more affordable options in smaller towns and rural areas.

For those who are certain about their choice of location and wish to invest in a permanent residence, purchasing property can be an attractive option. Spain's real estate market offers a wide variety of properties, from modern apartments and townhouses to traditional villas and countryside estates. Buying a home in Spain can provide a sense of stability and ownership, allowing you to personalize your living space and build equity over time. Additionally, owning property in Spain can offer potential financial benefits, as real estate in popular regions has historically appreciated in value. For retirees with family members who may wish to visit, having a permanent home provides a welcoming place where loved ones can gather and enjoy Spain together.

The process of buying property in Spain involves several steps, including selecting a property, negotiating a price, securing financing if needed, and completing legal and administrative requirements. Working with a reputable real estate agent who understands the local market and speaks your language can simplify the search and help you find a property that meets your criteria. It's also advisable to hire a lawyer who specializes in Spanish real estate law to assist with the legal aspects of the purchase, ensuring that all documents are in order and that the transaction complies with Spanish property regulations. This legal assistance is particularly important when buying older properties or rural homes, as these may have unique requirements related to land use, zoning, or historic preservation.

Once you have chosen a property, financing the purchase is a consideration for many retirees. If you are purchasing the property outright with savings, the process is relatively straightforward, involving a transfer of funds and the payment of associated fees. However, if you require a mortgage, Spanish banks offer financing options to foreign buyers, typically covering up to 70 percent of the property's value. Mortgage rates in Spain are competitive, but it's essential to compare offers and understand the terms, including interest rates, repayment schedules, and any associated fees. Some retirees may choose to secure financing in their home country, depending on currency exchange rates and lending options. Regardless of your financing method, having a clear understanding of your budget and the total costs involved in purchasing and maintaining a property is crucial.

In addition to the purchase price, owning a property in Spain incurs several ongoing expenses, including property taxes, community fees, and maintenance costs. Property taxes, known as Impuesto sobre Bienes Inmuebles (IBI), are set by local municipalities and vary depending on the property's location, size, and assessed value. Community fees apply to properties within shared complexes, such as apartments and townhouses, and cover the cost of maintaining common areas, such as pools, gardens, and building exteriors. Maintenance costs, including repairs, utilities, and general upkeep, should also be factored into your budget. These expenses are typically lower than in many other European countries, but understanding the full cost of ownership ensures that you can enjoy your property without financial strain.

Spain's real estate market is generally considered stable, but like any market, it can experience fluctuations. Coastal areas popular with expatriates may see seasonal demand spikes, especially in regions where tourism plays a significant role in the local economy. It's important to approach your property search with a realistic understanding of market conditions and the factors that can influence property values over time. Many retirees choose to work with a property advisor who can provide insights into local market trends, helping them make informed decisions about when and where to buy. With careful planning and due diligence, purchasing a home in Spain can be a rewarding investment that adds both financial value and quality of life.

Living in Spain as a homeowner or renter comes with certain cultural nuances and practices that may differ from those in your home country. For example, property ownership in Spain often involves joining a community association, known as a comunidad de propietarios, which is responsible for managing shared facilities and enforcing community rules. These associations typically hold regular meetings where owners can voice concerns, vote on budget allocations, and discuss maintenance issues. The sense of community that these associations foster can enhance the experience of living in a shared residential complex, but it's also important to be aware of the expectations and responsibilities that come with participation.

The architecture and design of homes in Spain vary greatly depending on the region and age of the property. Many traditional Spanish homes, particularly those in rural areas, are designed with thick stone walls and small windows to keep interiors cool in the hot summer months. These homes often feature distinctive elements, such as terracotta tile floors, exposed wooden beams, and central courtyards. In contrast, modern apartments in urban areas may have open floor plans, large windows, and contemporary finishes. Understanding these architectural differences can help you choose a home that aligns with your aesthetic preferences and comfort needs. Retirees who appreciate historical charm may be drawn to traditional homes with unique character, while those seeking convenience and modern amenities may prefer newer developments.

Once you have settled into your new home, Spain offers a lifestyle that is both rich in culture and focused on the enjoyment of daily life. The Spanish lifestyle places a strong emphasis on family, social connections, and outdoor activities, creating a warm and welcoming atmosphere for newcomers. Spanish culture encourages an appreciation for simple pleasures, whether it's a morning coffee in a neighborhood café, a stroll through a local market, or an evening gathering with friends over tapas and wine. This focus on community and enjoyment fosters a sense of belonging that many retirees find deeply fulfilling. As you integrate into your new neighborhood, you may discover that your neighbors and local business owners quickly become familiar faces, adding to the sense of home that your new residence provides.

In addition to the community-oriented aspects of Spanish life, Spain's infrastructure and public services make it a convenient and comfortable place to live. Spain has a well-developed transportation network, including high-speed trains, buses, and regional flights that make travel within the country easy and affordable. This accessibility allows retirees to explore different parts of Spain, from the historic cities of Seville and Granada to the coastal beauty of the Balearic Islands. Whether you plan to make regular trips or occasional excursions, Spain's transportation options make it possible to experience the country's diverse landscapes and cultural attractions without the need for extensive planning or expense.

The process of finding and settling into a new home in Spain is both an adventure and a journey of discovery. As you navigate the real estate market, explore different regions, and weigh the pros and cons of renting versus buying, you are gradually creating the foundation of your new life in Spain. This decision is not merely about choosing a physical space but about embracing a lifestyle that prioritizes well-being, community, and personal fulfillment. With careful planning, a clear vision, and an open heart, finding your new home in Spain can become one of the most rewarding experiences of your retirement journey, setting the stage for years of joy, relaxation, and exploration.

# Chapter 6
# Managing Finances in Spain

One of the most critical elements in planning for a successful retirement abroad is managing finances, and for those choosing Spain as their new home, understanding how to handle money effectively is essential. The financial landscape in Spain can differ greatly from what many retirees are accustomed to in their home countries, so preparation and knowledge are key. From establishing a local bank account and understanding the tax system to navigating currency exchanges and budgeting for daily expenses, managing finances in Spain requires a well-thought-out approach. Retirees who take the time to set up a solid financial framework can enjoy a stress-free retirement, making the most of their savings while also adapting to the Spanish way of life. In this chapter, we'll explore each element of managing finances in Spain to provide a clear path for retirees aiming to live comfortably and sustainably in their new surroundings.

The first step in managing finances in Spain is establishing a local bank account, which is essential for everyday transactions, bill payments, and integration into the Spanish financial system. Opening a Spanish bank account is generally straightforward, though the requirements can vary slightly depending on the bank and the type of account you choose. For retirees who are official residents of Spain, most banks require a residency card (Tarjeta de Identidad de Extranjero, or TIE), proof of address, and an initial deposit. Many banks in Spain offer specific accounts for expatriates, providing services in English and tailoring account features to suit the needs of foreign residents. These accounts often include online banking, international transfer options, and customer service in multiple languages, making it easier for retirees to manage their finances without a language barrier.

Non-residents can also open bank accounts in Spain, which can be helpful for those who are in the process of establishing residency or who plan to spend only part of the year in Spain. Non-resident accounts typically require a passport, proof of non-resident status (usually obtained from a local police station), and an initial deposit. Although non-resident accounts often have higher fees and fewer features than resident accounts, they provide a valuable bridge for retirees who are in the early stages of settling in. Many retirees start with a non-resident account and later switch to a resident account once they obtain their residency status, allowing them to benefit from better rates and more extensive banking services.

Spain's banking sector is well-developed, with a variety of banks to choose from, including national banks, regional banks, and international branches. Some of the largest banks in Spain, such as Banco Santander, BBVA, and CaixaBank, have extensive networks of ATMs and branches across the country, making them convenient options for retirees who need access to in-person banking services. Many of these banks also offer mobile apps and online banking platforms that simplify account management, allowing retirees to monitor their balances, pay bills, and make transfers with ease. Additionally, international banks like Deutsche Bank and Barclays have branches in Spain, which may appeal to retirees who are familiar with these institutions and prefer banking with a brand they know.

For retirees living on a fixed income or pension, currency exchange rates and international transfers are a major consideration. Spain's official currency is the euro, and retirees who receive income in a different currency, such as U.S. dollars or British pounds, must navigate the exchange rate to convert their funds into euros. Exchange rates fluctuate, so retirees should monitor these rates and consider using services that offer favorable exchange terms. Many banks charge fees for international transfers, which can add up over time, especially for those relying on regular pension or investment income. To minimize these fees, retirees may want to consider specialized foreign exchange services or online platforms that offer lower fees and competitive rates for currency conversions. These services can be particularly beneficial for those who need to transfer large amounts of money or who prefer to convert their income at specific intervals to take advantage of favorable exchange rates.

Understanding taxes is another essential part of managing finances in Spain, especially since Spain has a unique tax system that applies to both residents and non-residents. For retirees planning to spend more than 183 days per year in Spain, they are generally considered tax residents and are subject to Spanish taxes on their worldwide income. This rule applies to income from pensions, investments, rental properties, and other sources, which can have significant implications for retirees who have income from multiple countries. Spain has tax treaties with various countries, including the United States, the United Kingdom, and Canada, to prevent double taxation on the same income. These treaties allow retirees to claim exemptions or credits on foreign income, reducing their overall tax liability. Working with a tax advisor who specializes in Spanish tax law for expatriates is highly advisable, as the nuances of tax treaties and local regulations can be complex.

Spanish income tax rates are progressive, meaning that higher income levels are taxed at higher rates. The tax rate starts at around 19% for lower income levels and can reach up to 47% for the highest income brackets. Retirees should take these rates into account when calculating their post-tax income, as it may affect their budget and lifestyle choices in Spain. In addition to income tax, Spain imposes wealth taxes on individuals with assets exceeding a certain threshold. This wealth tax varies by region and applies to worldwide assets, including real estate, savings, and investments. For high-net-worth retirees, understanding and planning for this wealth tax is essential to avoid unexpected financial burdens. Some regions, such as Madrid, offer exemptions or lower wealth tax rates, so it's worth researching the tax policies in your chosen area.

Inheritance tax is another financial consideration for retirees who own property or have significant assets in Spain. Spanish inheritance laws differ from those in many other countries, and inheritance tax rates vary depending on the beneficiary's relationship to the deceased and the region where the assets are located. For instance, spouses and direct descendants generally benefit from lower tax rates and exemptions, while more distant relatives may face higher tax rates. To protect your assets and ensure that your estate is distributed according to your wishes, it's wise to consult with a legal advisor who can help you create a will that complies with both Spanish and international laws. Some retirees choose to establish trusts or other financial structures to minimize inheritance tax and ensure that their loved ones receive the maximum benefit from their estate.

Once you have set up a bank account, understood the tax implications, and arranged any necessary legal documentation, budgeting for daily expenses becomes a critical part of managing finances in Spain. The cost of living in Spain is generally lower than in many other Western European countries and North America, making it an attractive destination for retirees. However, living costs can vary significantly depending on the region, lifestyle choices, and individual needs. For example, retirees living in major cities like Madrid and Barcelona may face higher housing and dining costs compared to those in smaller towns or rural areas. Coastal regions, particularly those popular with expatriates, may also have higher living expenses, especially during the tourist season.

Housing is typically the largest expense for retirees, and the cost of rent or property ownership depends on location and property type. In popular coastal areas such as the Costa del Sol and Costa Blanca, rental prices for a one-bedroom apartment can range from 600 to 1,200 euros per month, while similar apartments in smaller towns or inland areas may cost between 400 and 800 euros. Property prices also vary widely, with homes in city centers and coastal areas commanding higher prices than those in rural regions. Many retirees find that owning a property in Spain can be more economical in the long run, especially if they plan to stay permanently.

Maintenance costs, utilities, and community fees should also be factored into the housing budget, as these expenses can add up over time.

Food and dining expenses are generally affordable in Spain, especially if you buy local and embrace the Mediterranean diet. Groceries, particularly fresh produce, bread, and olive oil, are reasonably priced and widely available. Shopping at local markets, known as mercados, is a popular and economical option for purchasing fresh fruits, vegetables, meats, and seafood. Dining out is also affordable, with many local restaurants offering a "menú del día" (menu of the day), a multi-course lunch at a set price that typically ranges from 10 to 15 euros. This offers retirees a cost-effective way to enjoy Spain's culinary delights without overspending. By balancing home-cooked meals with occasional dining out, retirees can enjoy a satisfying diet while keeping food expenses under control.

Transportation is another essential consideration for retirees, especially for those who wish to explore Spain's diverse regions. Spain has an extensive public transportation network, including buses, trains, and metro systems in larger cities, which makes getting around affordable and convenient. For example, a monthly public transportation pass in cities like Madrid and Barcelona costs around 50 to 60 euros, providing unlimited travel within designated zones. Retirees who prefer the freedom of driving can obtain a Spanish driver's license and either purchase or lease a vehicle. Fuel prices in Spain are moderate compared to other European countries, but car ownership entails additional costs, such as insurance, road taxes, and maintenance. Many retirees opt to use public transportation for city travel and rent a car for occasional trips to rural areas or neighboring countries, as this provides flexibility without the full costs of car ownership.

Healthcare is another key component of the retirement budget, and Spain offers a variety of healthcare options to suit different financial situations. Spain's public healthcare system, funded through taxes, provides high-quality medical care at a low cost for residents, making it accessible to retirees who qualify for residency status. While public healthcare is generally affordable, many retirees choose to supplement it with private health insurance to gain access to private hospitals, shorter wait times, and a broader range of specialists. Private health insurance premiums in Spain are typically lower than in many other Western countries, with basic plans starting at around 50 euros per month and comprehensive plans ranging from 100 to 200 euros per month, depending on coverage. This cost-effective healthcare system enables retirees to prioritize their health without excessive financial strain.

Entertainment and leisure activities are an enjoyable part of the Spanish lifestyle, and retirees will find that Spain offers a wide range of affordable options. From exploring historic sites and attending local festivals to enjoying outdoor activities like hiking, golfing, and sailing, Spain provides countless ways to stay active and engaged. Many cultural attractions, including museums and art galleries, offer discounted admission for seniors, and local community centers often provide free or low-cost classes and activities for residents. The cost of entertainment will vary based on personal preferences, but Spain's abundance of public parks, beaches, and cultural events ensures that there are plenty of options for retirees seeking budget-friendly leisure activities.

To manage finances effectively in Spain, it's helpful to develop a monthly budget that accounts for all major expenses, including housing, food, transportation, healthcare, and leisure. This budget should also include a cushion for unexpected costs, such as home repairs, medical expenses, or travel. Many retirees find that maintaining a detailed budget helps them live comfortably within their means, allowing them to enjoy the pleasures of Spanish life without worrying about financial stress. Additionally, it's wise to set aside a portion of your income or savings for future needs, as circumstances and expenses may change over time.

In summary, managing finances in Spain involves several key steps: opening a local bank account, understanding currency exchange and transfer options, navigating the tax system, budgeting for living expenses, and planning for healthcare and other essential needs. By approaching these aspects thoughtfully and staying informed about financial regulations, retirees can create a stable and enjoyable lifestyle in Spain. With careful planning and a clear understanding of your financial landscape, you can make the most of your retirement savings while embracing the Spanish way of life. A well-managed financial strategy will enable you to focus on what truly matters—building connections, exploring new places, and experiencing all that Spain has to offer.

# Chapter 7
# Adapting to Daily Life in Spain

Moving to a new country is an exciting adventure, but adjusting to a different culture and daily routine requires an open mind and a willingness to embrace change. For retirees relocating to Spain, adapting to daily life goes beyond simply learning the language or finding a place to live. It's about understanding the local customs, navigating the small but significant differences in daily routines, and gradually finding your place within Spanish society. Spain is known for its warm, relaxed lifestyle, and by taking the time to immerse yourself in this rhythm, you can discover a way of life that values community, leisure, and enjoyment in every aspect of the day. Adapting to life in Spain can be a transformative experience, offering retirees a renewed sense of purpose and a unique opportunity to live fully in the present moment.

One of the first aspects of daily life that retirees will notice in Spain is the distinct schedule that Spaniards follow. The Spanish day is often structured quite differently from what many newcomers are used to, with meals and social activities happening later than in many other countries. Lunch, known as "la comida," is typically served between 2:00 and 4:00 PM and is considered the main meal of the day. This is a time when families, friends, and colleagues gather for a hearty, multi-course meal that includes a starter, a main course, and often a dessert or fruit to finish. Lunch is followed by a period of rest known as the siesta, a tradition that originated in the hot regions of Spain and allows people to take a break during the warmest part of the day. While not everyone practices the siesta in modern Spain, particularly in larger cities where the pace of life is faster, the tradition still influences the general rhythm of the day, with many businesses closing for several hours in the afternoon.

Dinner, or "la cena," is typically a lighter meal and is served later in the evening, usually around 9:00 or 10:00 PM. This is much later than the dinnertime in countries like the United States or the United Kingdom, and it may take some time to adjust to this schedule. However, dining later in the evening has its own charm, as it allows for a more relaxed, social experience. Spaniards often spend several hours enjoying their meal, savoring each course, and engaging in conversation. The Spanish approach to dining emphasizes the importance of taking time to enjoy food and connect with loved ones, a tradition that many retirees find refreshing. Adapting to this new mealtime schedule can enhance your social life and deepen your connections within the community, as meals are often an occasion for friends and family to come together.

In addition to adjusting to mealtimes, retirees in Spain will notice the importance of community and social connections in daily life. Spaniards place a high value on relationships, and socializing is a significant part of the culture. It's common for people to greet one another warmly, even if they are strangers, and to engage in friendly conversation. Greetings are often accompanied by a kiss on each cheek, a gesture that may feel unfamiliar at first but is a meaningful expression of warmth and welcome in Spain. Over time, newcomers learn that these small gestures are an important part of integrating into Spanish society. By embracing the local customs and showing an interest in the lives of those around you, you can build friendships and create a strong support network that makes your life in Spain feel more complete.

Spanish society is also known for its respect for personal space and its relaxed approach to time, often referred to as "la hora española," or "Spanish time." Punctuality in Spain can be more flexible than in other countries, and people tend to prioritize personal interactions over strict schedules. If a friend is running late for a lunch appointment or a social event starts a little behind schedule, it's generally not seen as a big issue. This relaxed approach to time can take some getting used to, but it reflects the Spanish emphasis on enjoying the present moment rather than rushing from one task to another. Many retirees find that adapting to this relaxed attitude toward time allows them to let go of stress and focus on the joys of daily life, whether that means lingering over coffee with a friend or taking a leisurely walk through the neighborhood.

Another adjustment that retirees often experience when moving to Spain is the importance of learning at least basic Spanish. While it's possible to get by in larger cities and popular tourist areas with limited Spanish, knowing the language opens doors to deeper interactions and a richer experience of Spanish culture. The effort to learn Spanish is usually appreciated by locals, who are often patient and supportive of newcomers attempting to speak the language.

Spanish is relatively straightforward to learn compared to some other languages, with consistent pronunciation and a straightforward grammar structure, especially for those already familiar with Romance languages. Many retirees find that taking Spanish classes or participating in language exchange groups provides a sense of purpose and accomplishment, as well as an opportunity to meet other expatriates and locals who share their interest in language and culture.

Language aside, day-to-day life in Spain is also shaped by the country's rich calendar of traditions, festivals, and public holidays. Each region and even individual towns have their own unique celebrations that reflect local customs and history. Some of the most famous festivals in Spain include La Tomatina, where participants engage in a friendly tomato fight, and Las Fallas, a vibrant celebration in Valencia featuring elaborate sculptures that are eventually burned in a symbolic act of renewal. Semana Santa, or Holy Week, is another important tradition, particularly in cities like Seville, where processions and religious ceremonies honor Spain's Catholic heritage. Participating in or simply observing these events provides a unique insight into Spanish culture and history, and retirees who embrace these traditions often feel a deeper connection to their new home. These festivals and public holidays are a wonderful time to explore, make new friends, and fully immerse yourself in the Spanish way of life.

While Spain offers an affordable lifestyle, retirees will still need to adapt to new shopping and budgeting practices. In Spanish towns and cities, shopping for groceries and daily necessities is often done in smaller stores or local markets rather than large supermarkets. Spain's markets are a staple of community life, offering fresh produce, seafood, meats, and artisanal products in a vibrant and social setting. Shopping at local markets not only supports the local economy but also provides an opportunity to interact with vendors and experience the quality and freshness of Spanish ingredients. Many retirees enjoy the experience of visiting the market, selecting seasonal produce, and preparing meals with fresh ingredients that reflect the Mediterranean diet. In addition to fresh foods, Spain is known for its excellent wines, and local bodegas (wineries) often sell high-quality wines at affordable prices, adding to the enjoyment of everyday dining.

Transportation is another aspect of daily life in Spain that may differ from what retirees are accustomed to in their home countries. Spain has an extensive public transportation system, particularly in larger cities, where buses, trams, and metro services make it easy to get around without a car. Many retirees find that public transportation in Spain is affordable and convenient, allowing them to explore their new surroundings without the expense and responsibility of car ownership. For those living in smaller towns or rural areas, owning a car may be more practical, especially if public transport options are limited. Spain's road infrastructure is generally well-maintained, and driving is straightforward, though it's important to familiarize yourself with local traffic laws and road signs. Some retirees prefer to combine public transportation with car rental services for occasional trips, which provides flexibility without the costs of maintaining a vehicle year-round.

Healthcare access is another important part of adapting to life in Spain, and retirees will find that Spain's healthcare system is accessible and affordable. Spain offers both public and private healthcare options, with a high standard of care available across the country. Many retirees qualify for Spain's public healthcare system through residency, allowing them to access essential medical services at low or no cost. The private healthcare system, which is popular among expatriates, offers shorter wait times and access to private hospitals and English-speaking medical staff. Navigating the healthcare system in a new country can be challenging, but most retirees find that Spain's emphasis on patient-centered care and the availability of English-speaking services make the process manageable. Building a relationship with a local doctor, or médico de cabecera, can provide continuity of care and a sense of security, knowing that your health needs are well-supported in your new home.

Daily life in Spain also includes unique aspects of civic engagement and community participation. In Spain, many towns and cities have community centers, often called "casas de cultura" or "centros culturales," which offer classes, events, and activities for residents. These centers provide an array of opportunities, from language classes and cooking workshops to fitness programs and art exhibitions, all of which are designed to bring people together and enrich the lives of community members. Many retirees find these centers to be invaluable resources, as they provide not only a means of learning new skills but also a place to meet people and make friends. Spanish culture values lifelong learning, and retirees are often encouraged to continue exploring their interests and passions, whether through attending classes, joining clubs, or participating in volunteer activities that benefit the community.

Adapting to daily life in Spain also involves a gradual shift toward the Spanish lifestyle's emphasis on leisure and the enjoyment of simple pleasures. Spain's warm climate and beautiful landscapes invite residents to spend time outdoors, and many retirees find themselves naturally adopting a more active, outdoor-oriented lifestyle. From taking a leisurely walk in the evening, or "paseo," to enjoying coffee at an outdoor café, retirees have countless opportunities to relax and take in the beauty of their surroundings. Spanish towns and cities are designed to be pedestrian-friendly, with shaded plazas, parks, and scenic promenades that encourage people to gather, relax, and socialize. For many retirees, the Spanish lifestyle represents a welcome departure from the busy, achievement-oriented pace of life they may have experienced before, allowing them to focus on well-being, relationships, and the simple joys of daily life.

As retirees settle into life in Spain, they also become familiar with the country's legal and administrative processes, which are an essential part of everyday life. Spain has a well-organized system for managing residency, healthcare, taxes, and property ownership, but navigating these systems can require patience and organization. Many retirees find it helpful to work with a gestor, a professional advisor who specializes in Spanish bureaucracy and can assist with paperwork, appointments, and other administrative tasks. Gestores are knowledgeable about Spanish laws and regulations, and their services are invaluable for expatriates who may not be fluent in Spanish or who are unfamiliar with the intricacies of local procedures. With a gestor's assistance, retirees can handle administrative matters efficiently, freeing up more time to enjoy their new life in Spain.

In Spain, retirees will also discover a cultural emphasis on hospitality and generosity. Spaniards are known for their warmth and openness, and it's common for people to welcome newcomers with a friendly smile or an offer to join them for a drink. Social gatherings in Spain are often informal, and people are quick to include others, whether they are neighbors, friends, or even strangers. Retirees who show an interest in Spanish culture and a willingness to engage with locals often find that their efforts are met with genuine kindness and appreciation. This culture of hospitality extends to invitations to family gatherings, local festivals, and community events, providing retirees with countless opportunities to integrate into Spanish society and experience life as a local.

Adapting to daily life in Spain is a journey that unfolds gradually, as retirees learn to embrace new routines, connect with their community, and explore the richness of Spanish culture. This process may come with its challenges, such as adjusting to a different pace of life, learning a new language, or navigating cultural nuances, but the rewards are profound. Spain offers retirees not only a beautiful place to live but also a way of life that celebrates joy, connection, and personal fulfillment. By approaching this journey with curiosity, patience, and an open heart, retirees can create a meaningful and rewarding life in Spain, filled with friendships, experiences, and a deep sense of belonging.

# Chapter 8
# Embracing Spanish Culture

E mbracing the culture of a new country is one of the most enriching parts of relocating abroad, and for retirees moving to Spain, this journey of cultural immersion can add layers of meaning and enjoyment to daily life. Spanish culture is a vibrant mosaic, shaped by centuries of history, diverse regional influences, and deep-seated traditions that continue to flourish. From its expressive art and music to its warm social customs and lively festivals, Spanish culture offers a wealth of experiences that invite newcomers to join in and feel at home. Embracing this culture means more than observing its facets from the outside; it's about stepping into its rhythm, learning its stories, and finding ways to make Spanish customs, values, and traditions part of your own life.

One of the first aspects of Spanish culture that many retirees encounter is the importance of community and social connection. In Spain, people tend to prioritize relationships and value the time spent with family, friends, and neighbors. The social fabric in Spain is woven from a genuine sense of togetherness, and interactions with others are approached warmly and openly. This is evident in everyday encounters, where greetings are exchanged with affection and familiarity. Friends, family members, and even casual acquaintances greet one another with a "beso," a kiss on each cheek, and a friendly "¿Qué tal?" (How are you?) or "¿Todo bien?" (Everything good?). This openness is not merely polite; it reflects a deep cultural emphasis on the importance of social bonds. Retirees who take the time to engage in these daily interactions and show interest in others are likely to feel the warmth and acceptance of their Spanish neighbors, fostering a sense of belonging that can be both comforting and uplifting.

One of the best ways to embrace Spanish culture is through the country's culinary traditions. Spanish cuisine is a celebration of fresh ingredients, vibrant flavors, and regional diversity. Each region in Spain has its own unique dishes and specialties, reflecting the landscape, climate, and history of the area. In coastal regions, seafood plays a central role in the local cuisine, with dishes like "paella" from Valencia, which combines rice, saffron, and fresh seafood or meats, becoming iconic symbols of Spanish culinary culture. Inland areas are known for heartier fare, including stews, cured meats, and game. Andalusia, with its hot summers, is famous for "gazpacho," a refreshing cold tomato soup, while Galicia in the northwest is celebrated for its seafood dishes like "pulpo a la gallega," or Galician-style octopus. Sampling the local cuisine and learning to prepare traditional Spanish dishes can be a deeply satisfying way for retirees to connect with Spanish culture. Many towns and cities offer cooking classes or food tours, allowing newcomers to discover the techniques, ingredients, and stories behind Spain's most beloved dishes.

Food in Spain is not just about nourishment; it's also a key element of social gatherings and an opportunity for connection. Spaniards often linger over meals, engaging in conversation and savoring each bite. Lunch, or "comida," is typically the main meal of the day and often lasts longer than it might in other countries. Dining out is also an important part of Spanish social life, and retirees will quickly discover the joy of tapas, small plates that are meant to be shared. Tapas culture encourages sampling a variety of dishes while enjoying a relaxed evening with friends or family. Bars and restaurants across Spain serve a wide selection of tapas, from "patatas bravas" (crispy potatoes with a spicy tomato sauce) to "jamón ibérico" (Iberian ham) and "gambas al ajillo" (garlic shrimp). Trying different tapas and sharing food with others is not only a delicious experience but also an invitation to embrace the Spanish way of life, where meals are about more than food—they're a chance to connect, laugh, and unwind.

In addition to its culinary traditions, Spain has a rich artistic and musical heritage that offers retirees endless avenues for exploration and enjoyment. Spanish art and architecture are renowned worldwide, from the works of painters like Pablo Picasso and Salvador Dalí to the stunning architecture of Antoni Gaudí. Each city and town in Spain has its own architectural character, and wandering through the streets often feels like stepping into an open-air museum. In Barcelona, Gaudí's whimsical and surreal buildings, such as the Sagrada Familia and Park Güell, captivate the imagination with their intricate designs and unique use of color and form. In cities like Seville, Granada, and

Cordoba, the influence of Moorish architecture is evident in structures like the Alhambra, the Mezquita, and the Alcázar, where Islamic art and Spanish design merge in a breathtaking display of arches, tilework, and courtyards. Exploring these historic sites allows retirees to step back in time and witness the layers of history that have shaped Spain's cultural identity.

Music and dance are also integral to Spanish culture, and retirees who embrace these art forms can gain a deeper understanding of the Spanish spirit. Flamenco, a passionate and expressive style of music and dance that originated in Andalusia, is one of the most iconic symbols of Spanish culture. Flamenco performances are often an emotional experience, with dancers, singers, and guitarists conveying the raw intensity of joy, sorrow, love, and loss through intricate rhythms and movements. Many cities in Spain, particularly in the south, have flamenco venues where retirees can watch live performances and even take introductory dance classes to experience the art firsthand. Beyond flamenco, Spain has a vibrant music scene that spans various genres, from classical and opera to contemporary pop and rock. Music festivals, such as the Primavera Sound in Barcelona and the Feria de Abril in Seville, celebrate Spain's love for music and provide opportunities to experience the country's diverse musical landscape.

Spanish festivals, or "fiestas," are another essential part of the culture, providing an immersive experience that invites participants to celebrate local traditions, history, and community spirit. Spain is known for its lively festivals, many of which have been celebrated for centuries and continue to be a central part of Spanish life. One of the most famous is La Tomatina, held annually in Buñol, where participants engage in a playful tomato fight that leaves the streets awash in red.

Another popular festival is Las Fallas in Valencia, a week-long celebration featuring towering sculptures that are eventually burned in a dramatic spectacle, symbolizing renewal and rebirth. Semana Santa, or Holy Week, is a deeply religious and solemn celebration that takes place in cities across Spain, especially in Seville, where elaborate processions commemorate the Passion of Christ. Participating in these festivals offers retirees an opportunity to witness the vibrancy and diversity of Spanish culture, as well as to connect with locals and experience the joy and camaraderie that these events inspire.

The Spanish language is another gateway to understanding and embracing Spanish culture. While it's possible to navigate daily life in Spain without being fluent in Spanish, learning the language greatly enriches the experience. Spanish is the second most widely spoken language in the world, and acquiring even basic conversational skills can open doors to meaningful interactions and deeper friendships. Many retirees find that learning Spanish is a rewarding challenge that adds a new dimension to their lives, allowing them to engage more fully in their surroundings. Language schools, community classes, and online resources are widely available in Spain, offering accessible and flexible options for newcomers. Speaking Spanish not only facilitates practical tasks, such as shopping and navigating transportation, but also enhances the enjoyment of cultural events, festivals, and everyday interactions. Embracing the language is a gesture of respect that is often warmly received by locals, who appreciate the effort and are typically patient and encouraging with learners.

Religion and spirituality are also woven into the cultural fabric of Spain, where Catholicism has played a central role for centuries. Many of Spain's customs, festivals, and holidays have religious origins, and historic churches, cathedrals, and monasteries can be found throughout the country. These landmarks, such as the awe-inspiring Sagrada Familia in Barcelona or the Cathedral of Santiago de Compostela, are not only architectural marvels but also places of spiritual significance. While Spain is becoming increasingly secular, especially among younger generations, the influence of Catholicism is still visible in many aspects of daily life, from the celebration of saints' days to the traditional observance of Semana Santa. Retirees who are interested in spirituality will find that Spain offers a rich array of religious and spiritual experiences, from attending a mass in a centuries-old cathedral to exploring pilgrimage routes, such as the Camino de Santiago, which has drawn pilgrims from around the world for over a thousand years.

The concept of "fiesta" and "siesta" are also central to the Spanish way of life. While "fiesta" translates directly to "party" or "celebration," in Spanish culture, it embodies a broader approach to life that values joy, leisure, and togetherness. Fiestas can be official holidays, community gatherings, or informal social events, but the common thread is an emphasis on celebration and connection. Siesta, on the other hand, is a time of rest and relaxation during the hottest part of the day, traditionally observed in regions where the midday heat makes outdoor work uncomfortable. Although siesta is less common in bustling cities today, the practice still reflects Spain's cultural emphasis on balance and the importance of taking time to rest. Retirees who embrace the spirit of fiesta and siesta may find themselves feeling more relaxed, as these customs encourage a balance between activity and rest that supports both physical and emotional well-being.

Spain's culture also places a high value on family, which is central to social life and an integral part of Spanish identity. Family gatherings are common, and many families remain close-knit, with several generations living nearby or even in the same household. Family meals, Sunday lunches, and holiday celebrations are cherished traditions, and it's not uncommon for Spaniards to prioritize family over other commitments. For retirees living in Spain, forming friendships and bonds with local families can be a heartwarming experience, providing insight into Spanish values and a support network that feels like an extended family. Spanish hospitality is well-known, and many retirees find that neighbors and friends welcome them into their family gatherings, extending invitations to meals, celebrations, and other special occasions. This sense of family and community can be incredibly meaningful for retirees, especially those who may be far from their own families back home.

Nature and outdoor activities are also deeply ingrained in Spanish culture, as Spain's diverse landscapes provide endless opportunities for outdoor enjoyment. From the beaches of the Costa del Sol and the Balearic Islands to the mountains of the Pyrenees and the green valleys of Asturias, Spain's natural beauty is awe-inspiring. Spaniards have a deep appreciation for the outdoors, and activities such as hiking, cycling, and swimming are popular pastimes. The "paseo," or evening stroll, is a beloved tradition in Spain, where families, couples, and friends take a leisurely walk through the town or neighborhood after dinner. This daily ritual is not only a chance to enjoy the cool evening air but also an opportunity to connect with others and unwind. For retirees, joining the paseo is a simple yet enjoyable way to embrace Spanish culture, stay active, and feel connected to the community.

Embracing Spanish culture is a journey that involves discovering the nuances, values, and traditions that make Spain unique. This journey is not always easy; it requires an openness to change and a willingness to step out of one's comfort zone. However, the rewards of cultural immersion are profound, offering retirees a richer, more fulfilling experience of life in Spain. By participating in local traditions, learning the language, and forming connections with others, retirees can find a sense of belonging and purpose in their new home. Spain offers a lifestyle that celebrates the beauty of life's simple pleasures, and by embracing this way of life, retirees can create a vibrant and meaningful chapter in their lives. Embracing Spanish culture means more than just adapting to a new environment—it's about living with a renewed sense of joy, connection, and appreciation for the world around you.

# Chapter 9
# Staying Connected with Family and Friends

M oving to a new country like Spain is an exciting and transformative experience, yet it also brings unique challenges, especially for retirees who wish to remain connected to family and friends back home. Staying connected across distance requires intentional effort, thoughtful planning, and embracing new ways to communicate, but these connections are vital for maintaining emotional well-being and a sense of belonging. For many retirees, family and long-time friends are an essential part of their lives, representing shared histories, treasured memories, and a support system that cannot easily be replaced. Living in Spain need not mean a loss of these connections; rather, it presents an opportunity to find creative ways to stay involved in each other's lives, share in important moments, and maintain the strong relationships that enrich life.

One of the most accessible ways to stay connected with loved ones back home is through technology. Modern communication tools have made it easier than ever to bridge geograph-

ical distances, allowing for instant connections across conti-
nents. For retirees in Spain, using video-calling apps like
Zoom, Skype, and FaceTime provides a way to share face-to-
face conversations with family and friends, allowing for more
personal interactions than traditional phone calls or text
messages. Video calls can bring loved ones into your daily
life in a more intimate way, whether it's sharing a cup of
coffee over a morning call, giving a virtual tour of your new
home, or watching your grandchildren open birthday presents
in real time. Making video calls a regular part of your routine
helps you stay up-to-date with the lives of those you care
about and creates a sense of closeness despite the distance.

Social media also plays a valuable role in staying connected,
as platforms like Facebook, Instagram, and WhatsApp allow
you to share photos, updates, and messages with loved ones
in a more casual, ongoing way. For retirees living abroad,
social media can be a window into the daily lives of family
and friends, providing a way to celebrate milestones, see
pictures from family gatherings, and keep up with important
news. Social media also allows retirees to share their own
experiences, posting pictures of their travels, sharing updates
about life in Spain, and creating a shared digital space where
family and friends can stay engaged. WhatsApp is particularly popular in Spain, and using it to send quick messages,
photos, or voice recordings makes it easy to stay connected
on a day-to-day basis. Many retirees find that integrating
social media into their lives provides a sense of continuity
and connection, allowing them to feel part of family and
community moments even when they are far from home.

While technology makes it easy to stay connected, there's
something uniquely meaningful about maintaining traditional

forms of communication as well. Writing letters or sending postcards is a thoughtful way to show loved ones that they are in your thoughts, and these tangible reminders of connection can be treasured keepsakes. For retirees living in Spain, sending postcards from different regions or cities adds a personal touch, sharing a glimpse of your travels and adventures. Letters offer a chance to share your reflections, memories, and stories in a way that is often more intimate and contemplative than digital communication. Receiving a handwritten note or a postcard can be a delightful surprise for family members and friends, reminding them that they are still a cherished part of your life, even from afar.

Another important aspect of staying connected with family and friends is planning visits and reunions. Many retirees living in Spain look forward to hosting loved ones, and sharing their new life with family and friends can be one of the most rewarding aspects of the experience. Spain's appeal as a travel destination often makes it easy to encourage visits, and the chance to explore Spanish culture, history, and cuisine with loved ones adds an extra layer of enjoyment. Retirees can take pleasure in showing family members and friends around their town or city, introducing them to local customs, taking them to favorite restaurants, and creating memories in a place that has become home. Planning visits in advance allows both you and your guests to make the most of your time together, and it also gives you something to look forward to, knowing that you'll have the chance to reconnect in person.

For families with children or grandchildren, regular visits provide an opportunity for the younger generation to experience Spain firsthand, broadening their horizons and giving them a sense of the world beyond their own country. Children often find joy in exploring new places, trying new foods, and learning a few words of Spanish, making these visits an educational and enriching experience. Retirees can create special moments by organizing family activities, whether it's a day at the beach, a trip to a local museum, or an outing to a nearby vineyard or historic site. For grandchildren, spending time with grandparents in Spain can be an adventure, and these visits help build memories that will be cherished for years to come.

In addition to hosting visitors in Spain, many retirees make it a priority to travel back to their home country periodically. Regular trips home provide a way to reconnect with family and friends on familiar ground, attend important family events, and maintain ties with extended family members. Planning annual or semi-annual trips allows retirees to stay involved in family traditions, from holiday gatherings to birthdays and graduations. Some retirees find that combining visits home with family vacations or special outings creates a sense of celebration and ensures that each visit is meaningful. Traveling back home is also an opportunity to reconnect with old friends, share stories about life in Spain, and reinforce the bonds that have been part of one's life for decades.

For retirees who are unable to travel frequently due to health or budgetary considerations, establishing a regular communication routine can provide a sense of consistency and connection. Weekly or bi-weekly video calls, phone calls, or letter exchanges help create a rhythm that keeps family and friends close. Many retirees find comfort in knowing that they have a set time each week to catch up with loved ones, and this routine provides a sense of stability and continuity. Setting aside time for regular communication is especially important for retirees who may experience feelings of loneliness or homesickness. Having a reliable schedule of calls or virtual visits can alleviate these feelings and provide an emotional anchor in the midst of a new environment.

Embracing new traditions is another way that retirees can stay connected with loved ones while adapting to life in Spain. Holidays, family traditions, and cultural celebrations are important touchstones for maintaining connection, and retirees can blend their own traditions with Spanish customs to create a unique and meaningful experience. For example, while celebrating Christmas in Spain may differ from holiday customs in other countries, retirees can incorporate Spanish traditions, such as enjoying a Three Kings' Day parade or sharing Spanish treats like "turrón," while also including elements of their own holiday traditions. Inviting family and friends to celebrate these blended traditions during visits or sharing pictures and stories from these celebrations helps create a sense of shared experience, even when separated by distance.

In Spain, retirees also have the opportunity to forge new friendships and join social networks that expand their support system. Meeting new people and building friendships within the expatriate and local communities can provide additional sources of companionship, conversation, and connection. Expatriate groups, cultural organizations, and language exchange programs offer retirees a chance to meet others who share similar interests and backgrounds. Many retirees find that these new friendships not only enrich their lives in Spain but also create a network of support that makes it easier to stay connected with loved ones back home. New friends can offer advice, companionship, and understanding, particularly for those navigating the challenges and joys of living in a new country.

Volunteering is another meaningful way for retirees to stay connected while contributing to the community. By becoming involved in local volunteer programs, retirees can build relationships, share their skills, and make a positive impact in their new home. Volunteering can take many forms, from helping at a local charity, supporting environmental projects, or teaching English to Spanish-speaking students. These activities not only provide a sense of purpose but also foster connections with people of all ages and backgrounds, deepening one's involvement in the community. Many retirees find that volunteering helps them feel more rooted in Spain, creating a sense of belonging that complements their connections to family and friends back home.

As retirees adapt to life in Spain, they may find that their relationships with loved ones take on new dimensions, shaped by the experiences, challenges, and growth that come with living abroad. Embracing this evolution can be a positive and rewarding process, allowing retirees to share their journey with family and friends in a way that inspires curiosity and mutual respect. Sharing stories of life in Spain, from the beauty of the countryside to the intricacies of learning the language, allows loved ones to see the richness of the experience and appreciate the courage and adaptability it takes to live abroad. Retirees can be role models for family and friends, showing them that it's possible to pursue new dreams and challenges at any stage of life.

For many retirees, staying connected with loved ones while living in Spain also involves balancing independence with a sense of responsibility and involvement in family matters. While the move to Spain represents a new chapter of independence, retirees often remain actively involved in the lives of their children, grandchildren, and close friends. This involvement may take the form of providing advice, participating in important family discussions, or simply offering a listening ear during difficult times. By remaining available and supportive, retirees can maintain strong relationships and demonstrate that, despite the physical distance, they are still an integral part of their loved ones' lives. This balance between independence and connection allows retirees to enjoy the benefits of their new lifestyle in Spain while staying grounded in the relationships that matter most.

Retirees who are proactive about staying connected with family and friends often find that they experience a greater sense of contentment and satisfaction in their new life abroad. Maintaining these connections requires effort, but the rewards are immeasurable, providing a foundation of love, support, and continuity that enhances the experience of living in Spain. By combining technology with traditional communication methods, planning regular visits, and creating new traditions, retirees can keep loved ones close, even from afar. Building a fulfilling life in Spain doesn't mean leaving behind one's roots; rather, it means creating a life that honors both past and present connections, allowing retirees to feel at home in both places.

Ultimately, staying connected with family and friends is about nurturing relationships, sharing experiences, and celebrating life's moments together, no matter where you are. Spain offers retirees a unique and vibrant backdrop for this journey, with its welcoming culture, beautiful landscapes, and rich traditions. By embracing this new lifestyle while remaining connected to loved ones, retirees can create a balanced, fulfilling, and meaningful retirement experience that brings the best of both worlds into harmony. Spain becomes not just a new address, but a place where life continues to grow, evolve, and be shared with those who matter most, across all distances.

# Chapter 10
# Long-Term Considerations for Retirees in Spain

M oving to Spain for retirement is a thrilling venture, often filled with dreams of sun-soaked days, leisurely meals, and a more relaxed pace of life. But alongside the excitement of this new chapter, it's essential to consider the long-term aspects of living abroad, as they shape not only the practicalities of day-to-day life but also the potential for comfort, stability, and security in the years ahead. As time passes, retirees' needs and priorities evolve, and planning for these changes allows for a smoother, more enjoyable retirement experience. In Spain, a country that warmly welcomes retirees and expatriates, understanding key considerations such as legal planning, healthcare, financial stability, and aging-in-place services can significantly contribute to a peaceful and fulfilling long-term stay. Preparing for the future does not dampen the joy of the present; rather, it provides the foundation for a life in Spain that can grow richer and more resilient with each passing year.

One of the primary long-term considerations for retirees in Spain is estate planning, which includes wills, inheritance, and asset protection. Spain's inheritance laws and taxation rules differ from those in many other countries, so it's essential to develop a plan that aligns with both Spanish law and any applicable laws from your home country. Unlike some other countries, Spain practices what is known as forced heirship, meaning that a certain portion of an estate must be legally allocated to specific family members, typically children or spouses. This differs from countries where the individual has complete discretion over the distribution of their estate. While recent reforms have introduced some flexibility for expatriates, particularly those who wish to follow the inheritance laws of their home country, it's advisable to consult with a lawyer who specializes in international estate planning to ensure your wishes are carried out without legal complications.

Inheritance tax is another key aspect of estate planning in Spain. The tax rates can vary significantly based on the relationship between the inheritor and the deceased, as well as the region in which you reside. Direct family members such as spouses and children may benefit from reduced tax rates or exemptions, but extended family members or unrelated individuals may face higher tax liabilities. Each autonomous community in Spain has the authority to set its own inheritance tax rates, which can lead to significant variations across the country. Some regions, like Madrid, offer generous exemptions, while others impose higher rates. By understanding the specific rules in your region and planning accordingly, you can minimize tax implications for your loved ones. Many retirees find that working with an estate planner who is well-versed in Spanish tax laws and estate structures provides peace of mind, ensuring that their estate is managed in a way that honors both their legacy and the needs of their heirs.

As retirees consider their long-term finances, creating a sustainable financial plan is essential for a comfortable retirement in Spain. While the cost of living in Spain is generally affordable, financial needs and resources may change over time. Some retirees may wish to continue managing their investments from abroad, while others may choose to transfer their assets to Spain to simplify financial matters. Spain has tax treaties with numerous countries to prevent double taxation on foreign income, but the process of managing taxes, pensions, and investments in a new country can be complex. Working with a financial advisor who specializes in expatriate finances can help retirees develop a comprehensive plan that considers currency fluctuations, tax implications, and the long-term sustainability of income sources. For retirees who rely on pensions, it's wise to understand the conversion rates and any associated fees when transferring funds to Spain, as fluctuations in currency values can impact monthly income. By establishing a budget and planning for future financial needs, retirees can enjoy a more stable and worry-free lifestyle.

Healthcare is a critical part of long-term planning for retirees in Spain. Spain's healthcare system is highly regarded, with both public and private options that provide excellent care. For retirees who qualify for Spain's public healthcare system, the accessibility and affordability of medical services is a tremendous benefit. However, healthcare needs often evolve with age, and many retirees find that combining public healthcare with private insurance offers greater flexibility and shorter wait times for specialist appointments or elective procedures. Private healthcare allows retirees to access a broader range of services, including English-speaking doctors and international facilities that cater to expatriates. As medical needs may increase over time, it's worth considering the level of coverage provided by your private insurance and whether it includes benefits like dental care, vision, and long-term care.

For retirees with chronic health conditions or mobility concerns, planning for aging-in-place services is a thoughtful consideration. Spain offers various resources for elderly care, including home health aides, nursing services, and assisted living facilities. These services are available in both urban and rural areas, though options may be more limited outside major cities. Many municipalities provide services specifically for elderly residents, such as meal deliveries, transport assistance, and social programs, which can be invaluable for retirees who wish to remain independent while receiving support. Accessing these services often requires registration with the local municipality and a referral from a healthcare provider. Retirees who plan to live in Spain long-term may benefit from establishing connections with local support organizations, as these networks can be instrumental in finding resources and ensuring quality care.

In addition to healthcare and financial planning, another essential long-term consideration is the legal status of residency and the possibility of acquiring permanent residency or citizenship. Retirees who enter Spain on a long-term visa, such as the Non-Lucrative Visa or the Golden Visa, must renew their residency permits periodically, often for a period of up to five years. After five years of continuous legal residency, retirees may be eligible to apply for permanent residency, which offers more security and eliminates the need for frequent renewals. Permanent residency status allows retirees to enjoy the benefits of residency without the administrative burden of regular renewals, and it provides a level of stability that is valuable for those planning to spend the rest of their lives in Spain.

For retirees who feel deeply connected to Spain and wish to make it their permanent home, citizenship may be an option after ten years of continuous residence. Spanish citizenship offers a range of benefits, including the right to vote, travel more freely within the European Union, and access social services as a Spanish national. However, it's important to note that Spain does not permit dual citizenship for most non-EU nationals, meaning that retirees would need to renounce their original citizenship if they wish to become Spanish citizens. This decision is a significant one, and while citizenship can enhance a retiree's sense of belonging in Spain, permanent residency status often provides the level of stability that most retirees desire without requiring a change in citizenship. Each retiree's situation is unique, and consulting with a legal advisor can clarify the requirements, implications, and benefits of both permanent residency and citizenship.

Spain's tax system is another area that may require long-term planning for retirees. As tax residents of Spain, retirees are subject to Spanish taxes on their worldwide income, which includes pensions, investments, and other financial resources. Spain's tax rates vary based on income levels, and retirees should understand how these rates may impact their annual income. For retirees with significant assets, Spain also imposes a wealth tax, or "Impuesto sobre el Patrimonio," on worldwide assets above a certain threshold, with rates that vary by region. While some regions, like Madrid, offer wealth tax exemptions, others have more stringent tax requirements. Planning for these taxes with the help of a knowledgeable tax advisor ensures that retirees remain compliant with Spanish tax laws while optimizing their financial strategy. Proper tax planning can help retirees manage their income more effectively and avoid surprises at tax time.

For those with family abroad, planning for long-term family support and visits is another aspect of life that may require foresight. Many retirees wish to remain involved in the lives of their children, grandchildren, and other family members, and creating a plan for regular visits, family support, or potential relocation of family members can provide reassurance and continuity. Spain's status as a popular travel destination often encourages family members to visit, and some retirees choose to buy or rent properties that can accommodate guests comfortably. For those with family who may require more frequent support, arranging for family members to stay for extended periods or coordinating visits back home provides a sense of connection and involvement that helps mitigate the challenges of living abroad. Some retirees also explore the possibility of family reunification visas, which allow certain family members to join them in Spain, adding flexibility to family planning.

Another important consideration for retirees in Spain is adapting their home to support changing needs as they age. Spain's traditional architecture, particularly in older buildings, often includes features like narrow doorways, multiple levels, or steep stairs, which may become challenging over time. Retirees who plan to age in place may wish to make modifications to their home to ensure safety and accessibility. Simple changes, such as installing handrails, widening doorways, and adding non-slip surfaces, can make a home more suitable for mobility needs. For retirees considering purchasing a property, looking for single-level homes or homes with elevator access may provide added comfort and convenience. Spain also offers assisted living facilities and senior housing communities, particularly in urban areas, for those who prefer a supportive environment with access to healthcare and social activities.

A significant part of long-term planning is also understanding Spain's legal and healthcare directives, particularly regarding end-of-life care and medical decisions. Spain respects advanced healthcare directives, which allow individuals to express their preferences for medical treatment in the event that they are unable to make decisions for themselves. Retirees who wish to ensure that their healthcare wishes are respected can create a "Testamento Vital" (Living Will), which details their preferences for treatments, life-sustaining measures, and other medical decisions. Having these directives in place can ease decision-making for loved ones and provide retirees with peace of mind, knowing that their wishes will be honored. Similarly, appointing a healthcare proxy or representative, known as a "representante sanitario," allows retirees to designate someone to make medical decisions on their behalf if necessary.

Mental health and social connections are equally important considerations for retirees planning a long-term stay in Spain. As people age, social networks may naturally change, and maintaining a strong support system becomes essential for emotional well-being. Spain offers various resources for retirees to stay socially engaged, including community centers, cultural groups, and language exchange programs that bring people together. Many retirees also join expatriate organizations, clubs, and social groups that offer companionship, support, and shared experiences. Staying connected with family and friends back home, as discussed in the previous chapter, remains a vital part of emotional health. By maintaining a balance between new social connections in Spain and longstanding relationships abroad, retirees can create a well-rounded social support system that sustains them through the different phases of retirement.

As retirees consider their legacy and contributions, volunteering or mentoring can provide a meaningful sense of purpose and fulfillment. Spain has numerous opportunities for community involvement, from teaching English and assisting in environmental projects to supporting local charities and cultural organizations. Volunteering not only allows retirees to give back but also creates a connection to the community that enriches the retirement experience. Many retirees find that sharing their skills, knowledge, or time provides a sense of purpose and keeps them engaged and active. Mentoring younger generations or participating in cultural exchange programs can also offer retirees a rewarding way to leave a positive impact, create lasting memories, and foster a sense of pride in contributing to their community.

Planning for the long-term in Spain involves a holistic approach that encompasses financial stability, legal arrangements, healthcare needs, social engagement, and family connections. While the future is always unpredictable, having a plan in place provides retirees with the peace of mind and freedom to fully enjoy each day. With careful consideration and thoughtful preparation, retirees can embrace the present with confidence, knowing that their future in Spain is secure and well-supported. For retirees who have chosen Spain as their home, these long-term considerations are not only practical but also contribute to a sense of belonging and fulfillment, allowing them to savor the many joys of retirement in this beautiful country.

# Chapter 11
# Health, Wellness, and Lifestyle in Spain

Retirement is a unique opportunity to focus on health, wellness, and lifestyle choices that support a balanced and fulfilling life. For retirees moving to Spain, the country's warm climate, active lifestyle, and renowned healthcare system provide an ideal backdrop for a lifestyle that promotes both physical and mental well-being. Spain's approach to health and wellness aligns naturally with a philosophy that prioritizes balance, pleasure, and community, all essential aspects of living well in retirement. By immersing themselves in this lifestyle, retirees can discover a renewed sense of vitality and purpose, allowing them to make the most of their years in Spain.

Spain's Mediterranean climate is one of its most alluring features, particularly for retirees coming from colder or less temperate regions. The country enjoys long summers, mild winters, and ample sunshine, creating an inviting environment for outdoor activities year-round. Sunlight is known for its positive impact on mood, and Spain's sunny weather is often associated with a relaxed, cheerful atmosphere. The abundance of natural light, coupled with the vibrant colors of the Spanish landscape, contributes to a sense of well-being that can be invigorating. Many retirees find that their health improves simply by spending more time outdoors, breathing fresh air, and soaking up the sunshine. Whether strolling along a beach, exploring scenic mountain paths, or sitting in a plaza watching the world go by, the Spanish climate encourages people to slow down, unwind, and enjoy the beauty around them.

Spain's lifestyle is famously active, with many locals embracing physical activities as an integral part of daily life. This approach to movement and exercise fits well with retirement goals focused on health and longevity. Walking, or "el paseo," is a common activity, especially in the evenings when the heat of the day begins to wane. Spanish towns and cities are designed to be walkable, with pedestrian-friendly streets, shaded parks, and scenic promenades that invite residents to take a leisurely stroll. For retirees, the tradition of evening walks offers not only a low-impact form of exercise but also a way to socialize, meet neighbors, and observe the life of the community. This simple practice can be profoundly grounding and serves as a reminder to slow down and enjoy each moment, an approach that defines much of Spanish culture.

For those who enjoy more vigorous forms of exercise, Spain offers an array of options that cater to all fitness levels. Hiking is a popular pastime, and Spain's diverse terrain provides endless trails to explore. The Pyrenees, Sierra Nevada, and Picos de Europa offer breathtaking mountain landscapes for those who enjoy a challenge, while coastal trails along the Mediterranean or Atlantic provide scenic views with gentler inclines. Many retirees find that hiking in

Spain is not only a great way to stay fit but also an opportunity to connect with nature and explore the country's natural beauty. Cycling is another beloved activity in Spain, and many towns and cities have dedicated bike paths. The country also hosts several cycling events and races, including parts of the famous Vuelta a España, one of the world's premier cycling competitions. Even for retirees who are not competitive, cycling offers an enjoyable way to travel short distances, explore new areas, and maintain cardiovascular health.

Spain's beaches are a major attraction, and retirees who enjoy swimming, snorkeling, or simply relaxing by the water will find ample opportunities for beach outings. The Mediterranean Sea along the eastern coast offers calm, warm waters ideal for swimming, while the Atlantic coast provides cooler temperatures and stronger waves, attracting surfers and water sports enthusiasts. The beaches themselves vary from bustling city beaches with nearby restaurants and amenities to secluded coves and natural beaches that offer peace and solitude. Spending time at the beach is a cherished part of Spanish life, and for retirees, beach outings can become a regular part of their wellness routine, offering both physical exercise and relaxation. Many coastal areas also offer water aerobics classes, yoga on the beach, and other fitness activities designed for seniors, allowing retirees to stay active in an enjoyable, social setting.

The Mediterranean diet, widely considered one of the healthiest diets in the world, is another aspect of Spanish life that supports health and wellness. This diet emphasizes fresh fruits and vegetables, whole grains, legumes, lean proteins, and healthy fats, particularly olive oil. In Spain, food is often sourced locally and prepared simply, allowing the natural flavors and nutritional value of ingredients to shine. Fish and seafood are staples in Spanish cuisine, providing a source of omega-3 fatty acids, which are beneficial for heart health. Seasonal produce, such as tomatoes, peppers, and leafy greens, adds color and variety to meals, while dishes like "gazpacho" and "ensalada mixta" showcase the freshness and simplicity of the Mediterranean approach. Many retirees find that they naturally adopt the Mediterranean diet upon moving to Spain, enjoying not only the health benefits but also the pleasure of preparing and sharing flavorful, wholesome meals.

In Spain, meals are more than a time to eat; they are a social ritual that encourages connection and enjoyment. Spaniards tend to eat their meals more slowly than people in other countries, savoring each bite and often engaging in lively conversation. Dining is considered an experience to be shared, and whether it's a casual lunch at a local café or a festive dinner with friends and family, meals in Spain are a time to relax and engage. This approach to dining aligns with wellness principles that advocate mindful eating, promoting better digestion, reduced stress, and a sense of gratitude for the food and company. Many retirees discover that this slower, more intentional way of eating improves their overall well-being and adds a sense of fulfillment to their daily routine.

For retirees interested in wellness beyond diet and exercise, Spain offers a range of holistic health practices that complement traditional healthcare. Yoga, Pilates, and meditation are popular in Spain, and many cities have studios and wellness centers that offer classes in multiple languages. Yoga retreats are common, particularly in scenic areas like the Balearic Islands and the Costa Brava, where practitioners can enjoy classes overlooking the sea or surrounded by nature. Meditation and mindfulness practices are also embraced in Spain, and retirees seeking mental clarity and relaxation may find these practices to be a valuable addition to their wellness routine. Engaging in these holistic practices supports both physical and mental health, offering tools for relaxation, stress reduction, and personal growth.

Spain's spa culture is another delightful aspect of wellness, with numerous spas and wellness centers offering treatments that range from thermal baths to massages and hydrotherapy. Many of these spas are located in areas known for their natural mineral waters, such as Archena, Mondariz, and Lanjarón, where the water is believed to have healing properties. Thermal baths have been part of Spanish culture since Roman times, and the tradition of soaking in warm, mineral-rich waters is both relaxing and therapeutic. Retirees can enjoy these spa treatments to relieve tension, improve circulation, and experience a sense of renewal. Some spas offer packages designed specifically for seniors, including gentle massages, skin treatments, and therapies that cater to common health concerns associated with aging.

Social connection is a fundamental part of wellness, and Spain's culture places a high value on relationships and community. In Spain, friendships are nurtured and cherished, and social gatherings are a regular part of life. Retirees in Spain often find that socializing with friends, attending community events, and joining local clubs and groups contributes significantly to their sense of well-being. Spain's "tertulia" culture, or informal gatherings where people come together to discuss topics of interest, is a wonderful way for retirees to make connections and engage in meaningful conversations. Whether it's meeting friends for a coffee, attending a cultural event, or participating in a book club, the emphasis on community creates a supportive environment where retirees can feel valued and connected.

Mental health is an important aspect of wellness, and Spain's emphasis on balance, relaxation, and community can be beneficial for retirees navigating the psychological aspects of aging. Retirement often brings significant changes, including shifts in identity, purpose, and social networks. For retirees, staying mentally active and engaged is essential, and Spain provides a stimulating environment that encourages lifelong learning and personal growth. Many retirees take advantage of local language classes, cultural workshops, and educational programs, which offer both mental stimulation and a sense of accomplishment. Learning new skills, such as Spanish cooking, dancing, or painting, fosters creativity and provides a sense of purpose. These activities not only enrich retirees' lives but also contribute to mental resilience, allowing them to adapt to the changes that come with retirement.

Spiritual well-being is another dimension of health that retirees in Spain may wish to explore. Spain's rich spiritual heritage offers numerous opportunities for reflection, connection, and personal growth. While Spain is traditionally Catholic, the country is increasingly diverse, and retirees can find communities that align with a range of spiritual beliefs and practices. Attending services in a historic cathedral, walking part of the Camino de Santiago, or participating in a meditation retreat are all ways that retirees can deepen their spiritual life in Spain. The Camino de Santiago, a historic pilgrimage route, is particularly popular among retirees seeking a meaningful journey of self-discovery. The experience of walking the Camino, meeting fellow pilgrims, and connecting with nature can be transformative, providing a sense of inner peace and purpose.

Retirement in Spain also offers a chance to reflect on the concept of aging with dignity and purpose. Spanish culture places a high value on respecting and honoring elders, and retirees often find that they are welcomed and valued in the community. This cultural respect for age contributes to a positive self-image for retirees, reinforcing the idea that aging is a natural and valued part of life. Many retirees in Spain feel that they can age gracefully, without the pressure to conform to youth-centric standards, allowing them to fully embrace their stage in life. Engaging with younger generations, whether through family gatherings, community events, or volunteer work, also provides a sense of purpose and connection, reminding retirees that they continue to play an important role in society.

As retirees build their new life in Spain, creating a routine that includes both structured activities and unstructured leisure can enhance their sense of balance and well-being. A daily routine that combines physical activity, social connection, mental engagement, and relaxation supports overall health and makes each day more enjoyable. Many retirees find that having a flexible yet intentional routine provides a sense of stability, especially in a new environment. Spain's pace of life encourages this approach, as people are encouraged to enjoy both work and leisure, making time for rest and reflection. For retirees, this rhythm of activity and relaxation creates a balanced lifestyle that supports health and happiness.

Finally, wellness in retirement is also about finding joy and pursuing passions. Spain's culture encourages people to live fully, embracing experiences that bring pleasure and fulfillment. For retirees, this may mean exploring interests that were set aside during their working years, such as painting, writing, or playing music. Spain's art studios, galleries, music schools, and cultural centers provide countless opportunities to pursue creative passions and discover new talents. The country's rich artistic heritage serves as an inspiration, encouraging retirees to engage with the arts and find personal expression in their daily lives. Engaging in creative pursuits not only brings joy but also promotes mental and emotional well-being, making it an essential part of a fulfilling retirement.

Living in Spain offers retirees a holistic approach to health and wellness that encompasses physical activity, social connection, mental stimulation, and personal growth. Embracing the Spanish lifestyle, with its focus on balance, pleasure, and community, allows retirees to thrive in an environment that nurtures both body and spirit. By exploring the many dimensions of wellness—through diet, exercise, social engagement, spiritual growth, and creative pursuits—retirees in Spain can build a life that is not only healthy but also deeply satisfying. Each day becomes an opportunity to celebrate life, enjoy the beauty of the moment, and connect with others, creating a retirement experience that is as enriching as it is joyful.

## Chapter 12
# Reflections and Embracing the Journey

Retirement is a time for reinvention, reflection, and renewal, and for those who choose to retire in Spain, it is also a chance to embrace a new way of life that offers both challenges and rewards. Moving to another country to live out one's golden years is a monumental decision, one that brings the promise of adventure and transformation. By leaving behind familiar surroundings, retirees open themselves to the unexpected joys, cultural discoveries, and personal growth that living in Spain brings. However, alongside these wonderful experiences, there are also inevitable moments of homesickness, adaptation, and change. Embracing the journey of retirement in Spain means allowing oneself to be vulnerable, open to new connections, and committed to finding fulfillment in a foreign land. Reflecting on the steps taken to make this journey possible highlights the courage and resilience it takes to build a meaningful life abroad.

Reflecting on the decision to move to Spain often brings retirees back to the motivations that guided them in the first place: the desire for a slower, more enjoyable pace of life, the allure of a sunny Mediterranean climate, and the dream of experiencing a culture that celebrates community, food, and family. These motivations often serve as a foundation, helping retirees stay grounded when they encounter challenges or when the adjustment feels overwhelming. Spain's lifestyle offers simplicity and warmth, allowing retirees to savor everyday moments and engage with the world around them in new ways. For many, this shift in perspective brings a sense of freedom and contentment that was difficult to achieve in their previous lives. Life in Spain encourages a focus on quality over quantity, prompting retirees to let go of the need for constant productivity and embrace the beauty of being present. This new outlook fosters personal growth and a reconnection with oneself that can be transformative.

While life in Spain brings about positive changes, it also requires patience, flexibility, and a willingness to adapt. Moving to a new country comes with a learning curve that includes understanding local customs, navigating bureaucracy, and sometimes grappling with the language barrier. Retirees who reflect on these challenges often recognize them as essential parts of the journey, contributing to a stronger sense of self-reliance and resilience. Each hurdle becomes an opportunity to learn, whether it's mastering the intricacies of Spanish bureaucracy or overcoming cultural misunderstandings. In time, retirees develop confidence in their ability to handle whatever Spain throws their way, from unexpected paperwork to the occasional language mix-up. This adaptability often leads to a profound sense of accomplishment, as retirees realize that they are capable of thriving in a foreign environment and building a life on their own terms.

One of the most rewarding aspects of retiring in Spain is the chance to become part of a new community and experience a culture that values connection. Spain is a country that celebrates togetherness, and retirees who open themselves up to social opportunities find that Spanish culture warmly welcomes them. This sense of community is woven into daily life, from the friendly greetings exchanged in the local market to the gatherings that bring neighbors together over food and laughter. Retirees who reflect on their experiences often find that some of their most meaningful memories involve these small, seemingly ordinary moments. Forming friendships, sharing meals, and participating in local traditions create a sense of belonging that transcends nationality, making retirees feel like they are truly at home in Spain. These relationships become anchors, providing comfort and support in times of need and enhancing the joy of everyday experiences.

Spain also offers retirees the chance to cultivate a life filled with purpose and passion. Retirement can be an opportunity to revisit old interests or pursue new hobbies, and Spain's rich cultural landscape provides endless opportunities for exploration. Some retirees discover a love for Spanish cuisine and spend their days experimenting with local ingredients, learning recipes, and sharing meals with friends. Others may be drawn to Spanish art, finding inspiration in the works of great painters like Velázquez, Goya, and Picasso, or taking up painting themselves in the style of these masters. The freedom to explore these interests without the pressures of work or time constraints allows retirees to engage deeply with their passions, fostering a sense of fulfillment that enhances their quality of life. In Spain, the arts are accessible and celebrated, making it easy for retirees to find workshops, classes, and cultural events that nurture their creative spirit.

The journey of retirement in Spain is not only about embracing the external beauty and charm of the country but also about the internal journey of self-discovery and personal growth. Many retirees find that living in Spain brings out qualities they may not have recognized in themselves before. The challenges and joys of life abroad often spark a newfound sense of resilience, adaptability, and openness to the unexpected. Living in a foreign culture encourages retirees to let go of rigid expectations, appreciate the moment, and remain curious about the world around them. For some, this period of life becomes a kind of "second youth," a time when they feel free to experiment, take risks, and explore aspects of themselves that were previously overshadowed by work or family responsibilities. This personal growth becomes one of the most rewarding aspects of retirement in Spain, allowing retirees to redefine themselves and create a life that feels truly authentic.

While Spain offers much to retirees, there are times when they may experience a sense of longing for the familiar. Homesickness is a natural part of living abroad, especially during holidays, family milestones, or moments of solitude. Retirees who reflect on these feelings often recognize them as a testament to the deep connections they maintain with their loved ones and their past. Many find that staying connected with family and friends through technology, visits, or letters helps alleviate these feelings, allowing them to remain close to the people who matter most. Others find comfort in building new traditions that blend their past with their present, such as celebrating familiar holidays with a Spanish twist or sharing Spanish customs with family when they visit. These efforts to bridge the gap between their old and new lives bring a sense of continuity and belonging that enriches their experience in Spain.

The simplicity of life in Spain encourages retirees to focus on their health and well-being in a holistic way. Spain's lifestyle emphasizes balance, encouraging people to enjoy life's pleasures without excess. For retirees, this approach often leads to better health and a greater sense of well-being. The Mediterranean diet, abundant in fresh produce, olive oil, and seafood, supports a healthy body, while Spain's emphasis on leisure and relaxation contributes to mental wellness. Many retirees find that they experience less stress in Spain, as the pace of life is slower, and there is less emphasis on the hustle and bustle that often characterizes other cultures. This peaceful environment creates space for retirees to reflect on their health, develop new habits, and prioritize activities that contribute to their overall well-being. From regular exercise, like walking or swimming, to spending time with friends and family, the Spanish lifestyle provides a foundation for healthy aging.

Retirement in Spain also invites retirees to think about their legacy and the impact they wish to have on the world around them. With newfound time and freedom, many retirees choose to volunteer, mentor younger generations, or engage in community service, finding joy in giving back. Spain's strong sense of community and respect for elders make it an ideal place for retirees to contribute their time, wisdom, and skills in meaningful ways. Whether it's helping with local environmental projects, teaching English, or participating in cultural preservation initiatives, retirees find that these activities not only benefit their communities but also give them a profound sense of purpose. These acts of service become part of their legacy, creating a ripple effect that extends beyond their immediate surroundings and leaves a lasting impression on the people and places they care about.

Reflecting on the entire journey—from the initial decision to retire abroad to the everyday routines that shape life in Spain —reveals the courage and determination required to make such a transformative change. For retirees, the decision to move to Spain is often a leap of faith, one that involves leaving behind the security of the familiar for the promise of something new. Looking back, many retirees find that the journey has been worth it, as they have gained a deeper appreciation for life, a stronger sense of self, and a broader perspective on the world. The experience of living in a foreign culture, learning a new language, and building a life from the ground up fosters resilience and adaptability. This journey, filled with growth and discovery, becomes a testament to the strength and spirit of those who choose to make Spain their home.

In the end, retirement in Spain is about more than simply relocating; it is about crafting a lifestyle that resonates with one's deepest values and desires. Spain's culture, climate, and community offer a unique setting for this journey, providing retirees with the tools and environment needed to live fully and joyfully. For retirees, Spain is a place where they can explore, connect, and rediscover themselves, building a life that is rich in experiences, friendships, and memories. Embracing the journey means welcoming both the highs and lows, allowing oneself to grow through challenges, and savoring the moments of peace and joy that come from living authentically. This journey of retirement in Spain is not simply an ending but a new beginning, a chance to live with intention, gratitude, and a renewed sense of wonder.

# Afterword
## A Life Well Lived in Spain

Retiring to Spain is not simply about changing locations; it is about embracing a new chapter in life that balances tradition with the excitement of change, comfort with discovery, and connection with personal growth. For retirees, this journey to a foreign land brings the opportunity to reinvent and rediscover themselves in a setting that has welcomed countless people from all over the world. From the golden beaches of the Mediterranean coast to the lively plazas of Madrid, the cobblestone streets of quaint villages, and the green hills of the northern regions, Spain is a country of stunning diversity and contrast. It's a place where past and present coexist harmoniously, where life moves at a pace that invites reflection, and where community is valued in ways that create a sense of belonging even for those far from their original homes.

Spain's appeal to retirees is rooted not only in its climate, cuisine, and cost of living but also in its very ethos—a philosophy that values simplicity, enjoyment, and togetherness. In Spain, life is not measured solely by professional milestones or material achievements but by the quality of relationships, the pleasure of daily rituals, and the beauty of shared experiences. It is a country that invites newcomers to put down roots, to live intentionally, and to savor each day as it comes. Retirees in Spain find themselves embracing a new rhythm, one that aligns with their desire for a fulfilling and enjoyable retirement. This alignment of lifestyle with purpose provides a foundation for health, happiness, and well-being that enhances not only the length of life but its quality and depth.

For many retirees, moving to Spain represents a long-held dream or a cherished ambition finally realized. The decision to leave behind familiar surroundings, routines, and perhaps even loved ones is not an easy one, yet the rewards of living abroad are manifold. Spain offers the chance to encounter a vibrant and rich culture, to experience new traditions and languages, and to see the world through a fresh lens. These experiences offer retirees a chance to continually learn, grow, and challenge themselves. In Spain, every day holds the potential for discovery, whether it's in the laughter shared over a leisurely meal, the joy of meeting new friends, or the satisfaction of mastering a few more phrases in Spanish. This daily sense of possibility creates a feeling of vitality that energizes retirees and keeps them engaged, inspired, and active.

Living in Spain invites retirees to cultivate a life that balances leisure with activity, solitude with social connection, and routine with adventure. Many retirees find that, in Spain, they are able to achieve a balance that might have eluded them in their earlier lives. The Spanish lifestyle encourages one to slow down and appreciate the present moment. Morning coffee on a sun-drenched terrace, afternoon walks along the seafront, and evenings filled with tapas and conversation all create a daily rhythm that celebrates the small pleasures of life. This approach to living enhances mental and physical health by reducing stress, fostering meaningful interactions, and creating a foundation for personal well-being. Spain's environment supports this balanced lifestyle, with its abundance of natural beauty, pleasant climate, and opportunities for physical activities that suit all ages and abilities.

Another aspect of retirement in Spain that profoundly impacts newcomers is the sense of community and belonging that the country offers. Spanish society places great importance on relationships and togetherness. Whether in the cities, small towns, or rural villages, people connect with one another in ways that foster trust, kindness, and mutual support. This sense of community is woven into the fabric of everyday life, from friendly interactions with neighbors to the regular gatherings in local cafes, parks, and plazas. For retirees, this atmosphere of community provides a comforting sense of inclusion, and many find that they are welcomed as part of the social landscape. Becoming involved in neighborhood events, attending community festivals, or simply engaging with others in casual conversations helps retirees create meaningful connections. These relationships not only alleviate feelings of loneliness or homesickness but also provide a support system that is especially valuable for those living far from their country of origin.

As retirees reflect on their time in Spain, many recognize that the country's culture has influenced them in ways they may not have anticipated. Spanish culture, with its emphasis on relationships, family, and community, often inspires retirees to focus on what truly matters in life. The Spanish approach to work and leisure, which values a healthy balance and respects personal time, encourages retirees to rethink their priorities and let go of the constant rush and productivity mindset that may have dominated their working years. This shift in perspective is liberating, allowing retirees to live more freely and enjoy life in a way that feels authentic and deeply fulfilling. For many, the experience of living in Spain becomes a transformative journey, one that brings them closer to their true selves and enhances their understanding of life's simple joys.

Spain's approach to health and wellness also aligns naturally with retirees' goals of aging gracefully and maintaining a high quality of life. The country's emphasis on the Mediterranean diet, physical activity, and social connection fosters a lifestyle that supports longevity and vitality. The Mediterranean diet, rich in fruits, vegetables, olive oil, fish, and whole grains, provides a foundation for heart health, brain function, and physical strength. This diet is not just a nutritional guideline; it's a cultural practice that underscores the importance of fresh, locally-sourced ingredients and mindful eating. Retirees find that adopting this diet not only improves their health but also enhances their appreciation for food as a source of pleasure and sustenance. Additionally, Spain's active lifestyle, which includes daily walking, cycling, and outdoor activities, supports physical health in a way that is accessible to people of all fitness levels. In Spain, wellness is integrated into the very fabric of life, making it easy for retirees to maintain their health and enjoy their golden years.

One of the most profound aspects of retiring to Spain is the opportunity for personal growth and learning. Living in a new country brings challenges, from learning the language to adapting to a different pace of life, but these challenges often lead to valuable insights and new skills. Many retirees find that learning Spanish becomes a rewarding endeavor, one that opens doors to deeper interactions and enriches their experience of the culture. Language learning at any age stimulates the mind, improves cognitive function, and fosters a sense of accomplishment. Retirees who embrace this challenge often find themselves more confident and adaptable, gaining a renewed sense of purpose and pride in their ability to navigate a foreign language and culture. Beyond language, retirees can explore other avenues of learning, from attending local art classes and culinary workshops to participating in historical tours and cultural events. These opportunities for growth keep retirees mentally engaged, curious, and open to new perspectives, making retirement in Spain a time of intellectual as well as personal enrichment.

Reflecting on life in Spain also brings an awareness of the importance of family and enduring connections. While retirees may live far from their children, grandchildren, and friends, technology has made it possible to stay connected across great distances. Many retirees find comfort in knowing that, even from abroad, they can remain a part of their loved ones' lives, sharing in family milestones, birthdays, and holidays through video calls, messages, and visits. Spain's appeal as a travel destination makes it an ideal place for family reunions, and retirees often delight in sharing their new home with visiting loved ones. Hosting family in Spain becomes an opportunity to create memories together, show their family the beauty of Spanish culture, and strengthen bonds that may be stretched by physical distance but are never diminished. These visits bridge the gap between old and new lives, allowing retirees to stay connected to their roots while fully embracing their life in Spain.

For retirees, the decision to move to Spain is also about legacy and the desire to create a lasting impact. Many choose to engage in volunteer work, community projects, or mentoring programs, finding purpose in contributing to the country that has become their home. Spain's openness to newcomers and its respect for the contributions of all ages provide an ideal environment for retirees to make a positive difference. Whether it's teaching English, supporting environmental initiatives, or participating in local charities, retirees find fulfillment in giving back to the community and leaving a legacy that reflects their values and passions. These contributions not only enhance the lives of those around them but also bring retirees a sense of accomplishment and pride in their ability to make a meaningful difference.

As retirees reflect on their journey to and within Spain, they often realize that this chapter of life has brought unexpected depth, joy, and understanding. Moving to Spain, with all of its challenges and delights, has allowed them to see life in a new light, one that values simplicity, presence, and connection. Spain's culture, climate, and people have shaped them in ways that go beyond the surface, influencing their outlook on life, their sense of self, and their understanding of what it means to truly live well. This journey of retirement in Spain is not only a testament to the courage and adaptability of those who choose to live abroad but also a reminder of the beauty and richness that life can offer when one is open to new experiences and willing to embrace change.

In the end, retiring to Spain is a decision to live life fully, to explore the unknown, and to embrace the present with open arms. Spain's warmth, charm, and spirit offer retirees a place to build new memories, pursue their passions, and savor the time they have. For those who have made Spain their home, each day is an opportunity to live intentionally, to celebrate the small wonders of daily life, and to connect with a world that feels vibrant, inviting, and full of possibility. This journey is a gift, one that allows retirees to rediscover themselves, to find joy in simplicity, and to experience a life well-lived in the heart of Spain.

The End

Made in United States
Troutdale, OR
12/15/2024

26546104R00070